verbatim
verbatim

verbatim verbatim

CONTEMPORARY DOCUMENTARY THEATRE

EDITED BY WILL HAMMOND & DAN STEWARD

OBERON BOOKS

LONDON

First published in 2008 by Oberon Books Ltd

521 Caledonian Road, London N7 9RH

020 7607 3637 / 020 7607 3629

info@oberonbooks.com / www.oberonbooks.com

Reprinted in 2010, 2011, 2013, 2014, 2016

A catalogue record for this book is available from the British Library.

PB ISBN: 978 1 84002 697 9
E ISBN: 978 1 84943 665 6

Design by Dan Steward

Printed, bound and converted by CPI Group (UK) Ltd., Croydon, CR0 4YY.

Visit www.oberonbooks.com to read more about all our books and to buy them. You will also find features, author interviews and news of any author events, and you can sign up for e-newsletters so that you're always first to hear about our new releases.

CONTENTS

INTRODUCTION

Albert Einstein once observed that 'The secret to creativity is knowing how to hide your sources.' The creative endeavour under discussion in this book, a style of theatre-making commonly referred to as 'verbatim', does the opposite. Instead of adapting or repackaging experiences or observations within a fictional dramatic situation, a verbatim play acknowledges, and often draws attention to, its roots in real life.

The term *verbatim* refers to the origins of the text spoken in the play. The words of real people are recorded or transcribed by a dramatist during an interview or research process, or are appropriated from existing records such as the transcripts of an official enquiry. They are then edited, arranged or recontextualised to form a dramatic presentation, in which actors take on the characters of the real individuals whose words are being used.

In this sense, verbatim is not a form, it is a technique; it is a means rather than an end. For this reason, *verbatim theatre* can be used to describe plays that are sometimes so dissimilar that the term may appear to be of little value. What does *The Crucible* have in common with *Black Watch* that is worth discussing? All they share is that their makers, Arthur Miller and Gregory Burke, have claimed, to a greater or lesser extent, that the characters who appear in them exist or have existed in the real world, outside of the theatre, outside of their imagination, and that the words those people are shown to be speaking are indeed their own.

This claim to veracity on the part of the theatre maker, however hazy or implicit, changes everything. Immediately, we approach the play not just as a play but also as an accurate source of information. We trust and expect that we are not being lied to. When this claim is made, theatre and journalism overlap, and like a journalist, the dramatist must abide by some sort of ethical code if their work is to be taken seriously. The makers of *Called to Account* must be prepared to be called to account themselves.

It also changes nothing. As David Hare argues, the fact that the people in his plays actually exist and the words in his plays were actually spoken by them in no way alters his role as a dramatist. The real world provides him with the raw material, which, as Max Stafford-Clark puts it, he leaves 'raw', but he must still craft a drama from it. The stone of Michelangelo's *David* is 'real' stone – he didn't make it himself – but the sculpture is no less the creation of his skill, imagination and hard work.

Nevertheless, the claim to veracity is there, and even David Hare and Max Stafford-Clark agree that they are bound, if only by their own sense of honour and integrity, not to misrepresent. No play, like no newspaper article, is without bias and inflection, but, Hare argues, people who work in the theatre tend simply to have much less to gain from lies and spin, and much more interest in being honest. This sort of theatre provides what journalism fails to provide, and at a time when it is sorely needed.

For anyone familiar with the history of 20th-century theatre, this isn't news. Erwin Piscator's 'living newspaper'; the instant street theatre of the Theatre Workshop pioneers; Peter Cheeseman's Stoke documentaries; Rolf Hochhuth's historical excavations; Anna Deavere Smith's one-person dramatisations: contemporary documentary theatre has a rich heritage to draw on. What does seem to be new, though, is verbatim theatre's recent rise to prominence and acceptance as a mainstream method in its own right. An element of chance and initial reluctance are a feature of several of these contributors' accounts, as they describe how they became involved with verbatim. Because of them, though, a new generation of theatre makers is now encountering verbatim plays on the great stages of their national theatres, on Broadway and in the West End, and they are actively choosing to make verbatim drama themselves. However loose and abstract our definition of it, verbatim is now being studied as a theatre genre. It has been filmed and aired on television. It has been performed in Britain's House of Lords. It is thriving. Why?

The content of plays such as *My Name is Rachel Corrie*, *The Colour of Justice* or *Talking to Terrorists* – the suffering of the Palestinian people, institutional racism and injustice, the global threat of terrorism – might suggest that we turn to verbatim theatre because we feel that it is somehow better suited to the task of dealing with serious subject matter. The world seems to have become a more serious place, and we want our theatre to help us understand it. Certainly, Nicolas Kent and Richard Norton-Taylor see their tribunal plays as providing an opportunity for non-experts to grapple with the detail of important public enquiries for themselves, and in the process, if they're lucky, to spur a powerful person into positive action.

But what about Alecky Blythe's *Cruising*, a play about the love lives of the elderly? Or Robin Soans's *Life After Scandal*, in which those who have suffered high-profile public disgrace describe their ordeal? These plays have 'serious' points to make, but verbatim seems also to offer a highly personal, confessional mode. Alecky Blythe relates this to our current obsession with manufactured celebrity. Anyone can be the star of a verbatim play. While the tribunal plays are lauded for being a tool for democracy, their purpose being to provide more people with greater access to important information, Alecky Blythe's plays are even more accessible to the public, and in a more literal sense: you can be in them. Looked at in this light, verbatim theatre is a remarkably democratic medium. Is this what attracts us to it?

For every fan of verbatim, though, there is a critic. *The Exonerated* tells of the deeply upsetting experiences of those condemned unjustly to death and later reprieved. Productions of the play featured performances by Richard Dreyfuss, Mia Farrow, Jeff Goldblum, Robin Williams and Stockard Channing. For some, this combination of suffering and celebrity highlighted the question of whether verbatim is inherently exploitative or voyeuristic. Dennis Kelly's play *Taking Care of Baby* is in part a play about this very debate. Questions that have been asked of reality TV are now being directed at the theatre.

The purpose of this book is to provide the reader with first-hand descriptions of a variety of approaches to making verbatim theatre, to celebrate that variety, and to explore the ways in which verbatim defies any straightforward categorisation. It also provides the contributors with an opportunity to address these and some of the other questions that it continues to provoke – questions of truth and integrity, reality and fiction – as well as questions about rehearsal, research, editing, stagecraft and performance techniques. The interviews and essays are each the culmination of several discussions. Collected together, they are intended to be a snapshot of verbatim theatre as it now stands and, we hope, a provocation to further debate.

ROBIN SOANS

Robin Soans's plays include *Life After Scandal*, *Talking to Terrorists*, *The Arab-Israeli Cookbook*, *A State Affair* and *Across the Divide*, all of which use verbatim techniques. As an actor he has worked in theatre, film, radio and TV.

The arts are more than mere entertainment. In my view they should also be the vessel which houses the conscience of a nation; they should ask the difficult questions others would rather leave unasked. In recent years, as those in power have grown cleverer and cleverer in news manipulation, the need to ask such questions has grown. It can be no accident that, as the art of spin has become more sophisticated, leading to a decline in standards of honesty in public life, there has been a simultaneous proliferation of political theatre. The phrase 'it does what it says on the tin' is much in fashion at the moment, yet it seems to me that we are living in an age when virtually nothing 'does what it says on the tin': photographs are faked; television competitions are won by people who haven't entered; articles in newspapers turn out to have been entirely fabricated; weapons of mass destruction cannot be found in Iraq. I am currently working in Burnley. Outside Burnley College, there is a huge sign announcing 'Burnley College…100 per cent pass rate for the second year running' – yet this 100 per cent pass rate is maintained by dismissing failing students at Christmas. The normal channels of reportage, wherein we expect some degree of responsibility and truth, are no longer reliable. Only in the arts is the study of the human condition considered more important than ambition or money, so it is left to artists to ask the relevant questions.

This is not the same thing as providing solutions. In his review of my play *Talking to Terrorists*, Paul Taylor of the *Independent* quoted Chekhov's statement that: 'The purpose of the theatre is not to provide the solutions, but to state the problems more clearly.' I accept this diagnosis: as a verbatim playwright, I interview people who have knowledge and experience that relates to the 'problem' under consideration, and edit their responses into a play. For me, stating the problems more clearly isn't just a case of asking interesting questions, it is also about widening the number and variety of people you listen to, to include people who traditionally haven't been seen and heard in the theatre. With someone in the public domain, the process involves persuading them to speak off the record, then really listening to them, not just going through the motions. Ultimately, stating the problems more clearly is a case of trying to give the audience a broader base of knowledge of whichever subject is being tackled. When we performed *Talking to Terrorists* at the Royal Court, the Anti-Terrorist Branch at Scotland Yard came to see the play and said they found it very informative.

How is this any different from a well-written and well-constructed imagined play? The answer is: it isn't. The categorisation is irksome. Verbatim plays are far more like conventional plays than is generally acknowledged – and, in fact, I think conventional plays are far more like verbatim than most people realise. Max Stafford-Clark once asked Andrea Dunbar why she ended a scene at a particular point, and she replied: 'Oh, they went round the corner. I didn't hear what they said next.' Alan Bennett told me that the curious incident on the pillion of the motorbike related in *The History Boys* actually happened to him. Hamlet's exhortation to his players to hold a mirror up to nature doesn't merely apply to actors. The writing that hooks an audience is full of moments of recognition; it relates to our own experiences. Whether this writing is the interweaving of transcribed conversations, or is constructed from episodes remembered in a playwright's mind, makes very little difference.

One of the main differences between 'created' and 'verbatim' plays lies in the expectations of the audience. The audience for a verbatim play will expect the play to be political; they will be willing to accept an unconventional format; they will probably expect the material to be contentious and to challenge their opinions. At least they will expect to be surprised by some of the revelations on offer. Simply by choosing to put a subject under the theatrical microscope, the playwright is saying 'There's more to this than meets the eye', or 'History relates this to be the case; I think it needs to be re-examined', or even 'I found this so interesting I would like to share it with you...it might change your opinions'. Above all, the audience for a verbatim play will enter the theatre with the understanding that they're not going to be lied to. They may be unsettled by the unusual way the play is constructed, but they will be compensated for the lack of convention by the assumption that what they are looking at and listening to is revelatory and truthful.

●

I never made a conscious decision to become involved in verbatim theatre. It happened by accident, but I suppose you could say it was an accident waiting to happen...

I blame much on my own personality. Although in my general conduct I have always been superficially affable, there lurks under the surface a deep well of non-conformity – and, I hope, a sympathetic awareness of the fragility of human nature. This started early. As a small boy I was marched off to church every Sunday. Being the posh family in the village, we sat in the front pew, and my father would read the lesson in a sonorous voice. When I asked if there was something un-Christian about the villagers being arranged in accordance with their social status, I was told this was not the sort of question I should ask, and that I should pray for forgiveness. My parents took to describing me to their friends as 'a bit of a red under the bed' because, from an early age, I refused to swallow their political leanings and social values without question. Later, my desire to become an actor was both a tactic to hide my social awkwardness and an act of resistance against the pressure to conform, and in my career I have mostly worked in the more political, less commercial sector of both theatre and film.

In the autumn of 1995, I was asked to take part in a rehearsed reading at the Royal Court of a verbatim play called *Waiting Room Germany*, by the German playwright Klaus Pohl. He had interviewed a number of people from what used to be East and West Germany about how their lives changed in the five years after the Berlin Wall came down, and had woven the material into twenty-three semi-poetic monologues and one duologue. A cast of five worked on the material for two days with the director Mary Peate, and then we gave the reading in the Theatre Upstairs. In the normal course of events, that would have been that.

The next show downstairs at the Court was *Harry and Me* by Nigel Williams, but halfway through rehearsals one of the actors dropped out. His part was recast and rehearsals continued, but the opening was delayed. The Court could have resigned itself to leaving the main stage dark for a fortnight; instead the plan was hatched to give *Waiting Room Germany* a full production. The reading had been a success and the set could be very simple, so it would be relatively cheap and easy to stage the play at short notice. We had ten days' rehearsal, and the play opened with very few fanfares, not many bookings and no great expectations of success.

Something became apparent in the last days of rehearsal. This was a particularly nerve-wracking form of theatre for the actors. Most performances have a geographical as well as an emotional and psychological shape: 'This is where I amble to the sideboard, laugh in a cavalier fashion, and pour myself a brandy.' There was none of that here. In *Waiting Room Germany* we spent most of the time sitting on chairs at the front of the stage talking to the audience. In Restoration Comedy, approximately ninety per cent of the actor's relationships are with the other actors on stage, and ten per cent are with the audience, in the form of asides. In verbatim theatre, the ratio is reversed: ten per cent of the time you interact with your fellow actors on stage, but ninety per cent of the time your attention is directed towards the audience. The audience becomes a key, if silent, character in the performance. The quintessence of verbatim theatre is a group of actors sitting on chairs, or cardboard boxes or a sofa, talking to the audience, simply telling stories. In my own verbatim plays I have tried to weave my material into scenes, to give the actors a geographic pattern and to get away from a landscape of monolithic chunks of talking. But the principal skill required of the actor remains that of the storyteller, and his or her key relationship is with the audience.

We were extremely nervous before the first performance.
None of us entirely trusted the material. Who was going to be
engrossed by a professor from Leipzig rejoicing in the fact that
he could now walk through the woods on his way to work? Or a
factory hand explaining that she now turned out parts for airbags
instead of nougat?

The doubt was short-lived. A few lines into my first long
monologue, I became aware that the audience was listening. And
not just listening, but *really* listening. After thirty years of acting
in plays, I know exactly when an audience is listening – and when
its various members are counting the beams in the roof, or looking
at their watches and wishing they were in a Thai restaurant eating
noodles. After just two paragraphs of text, they were deeply and
personally engrossed in the story. During my second monologue,
the account of a man who'd endured a great deal in striving for
the welfare of the town where he lived, I got to the point where
he said, 'Yesterday I submitted nomination papers, and I'm
going to stand for Mayor', and the whole audience burst into
applause. If there has been a defining moment in my induction
as a verbatim actor and dramatist, that spontaneous reaction
was it. I realised I had become involved in something rather
extraordinary. Not only were these people following my every
syllable, but they were emotionally bound up with me as well. In
all my years of acting, I had hardly ever had such keen attention
paid to me. My last monologue, which was a harrowing account
of survival against persecution, lasted over twenty minutes.
You could have heard a pin drop. This was obviously a potent
and relevant form of theatre, and I wanted to know more. The
audience were paying a different kind of attention to this play,
an unsophisticated attention which was new to me. What do I

mean by that? A large proportion of the audience at the National Theatre, where I had just been working, seemed to view the acting in much the same way as they might judge a cricket shot or discuss the pros and cons of a fine wine. After a monologue or particularly vibrant scene, I had often heard members of the audience shout out 'Well played!', as if David Gower had just elegantly stroked the ball to the boundary. If I can put it like this, for a majority of the audience there was a disinterested detachment, a metaphorical awarding of marks like the panel of judges at an ice-skating competition. They had cast themselves in the role of the connoisseur, so that a part of their brain was occupied with questions such as, 'Should I be finding this funny?' What intrigued me with *Waiting Room Germany* was that this layer of detachment had evaporated, and that the audience was unselfconsciously – that's the word, unselfconsciously – involved with the stories and the dilemmas of the characters telling it. This doesn't happen very often in the theatre, and it prompted me to wonder why this should be the case.

In verbatim theatre the audience assumes an active rather than a passive role. This also happens to a lesser extent during Shakespearean plays, when there are soliloquies, or Restoration plays, when there are asides – in other words, when the character confides in the audience personally. Suppose I went to interview Mo Mowlam. She talks to me; I write down her words, and then edit them into a speech, or in some cases into dialogue between her and her husband. We then cast June Watson in the role. She sits on a chair on stage and talks to an audience, just as the original Mo Mowlam talked to me. By this process, the audience have become me, or whomever I happened to be with when I conducted the interview, and the Mo Mowlam on stage talks to the audience on a purely personal and confidential level. Every member of that audience begins to feel, 'This woman is sharing the intimate details of her life with me...her hopes, her regrets, her dilemmas, her innermost thoughts... She's speaking off the record with a frankness that she could never show in her public life... She even reveals her penchant for broken biscuits.' Transferring a deeply personal conversation onto the stage in this way confers a responsibility on the audience – a responsibility which I think they enjoy – and this partially accounts for the increased intensity of their listening.

Further encouraging the audience's involvement must be the care they develop for the characters. How many times after a show have I heard people say, 'I didn't enjoy it very much; I didn't care for any of the characters'? The chief reason for this failure is that the characters seem somehow artificial and therefore difficult to relate to. Artificiality is a charge that cannot be raised against the verbatim playwright unless he or she is a complete charlatan. Actually, when the bricks and mortar of a play are real conversations, people use such idiosyncratic and bizarre language that it is immediately recognisable as lacking in artifice. I interviewed a paparazzo for my recent play on scandal, and he said, 'If someone's snorting cocaine or picking their nose, I'll leave that alone, but a lot of photographers are looking for that...crack-sweaty-arse-pants...zoom in on armpits, all sorts of crap.' I doubt many writers would or even could come up with the phrase 'crack-sweaty-arse-pants', but we know exactly what the photographer means; it has the undeniable ring of truth about it, as well as the sort of detail that is instantly recognisable and therefore binds us to the character. Once a writer has convinced the audience that they're privy to an actual conversation, the audience will be more willing to embark on the emotional or philosophical journey of the play – especially if they already feel that they're being addressed personally.

●

This is certainly what happened in *Waiting Room Germany*, which turned into quite a hit. Far from indifferent notices and an audience comprising two nuns and a dead wasp, the critics were impressed and the houses were full. I was sufficiently buoyed by the experience to think I might try to write an English equivalent.

My intention was to test the temperature of the political water in Britain at the end of John Major's government. We were at a watershed in recent political history: the Tories had been in power for a long time; the Socialists had been in the wilderness, but had found a new messiah who promised he had the key to power. I wanted to interview a cross-section of people about their political inclinations in the six months leading up to the 1997 election, but from a purely personal point of view: what mattered to them in their lives? What individual dilemmas, hopes and fears would influence the way they voted? Stephen Daldry, who was running the Court at the time, gave me some encouragement in this. 'But you need to give it form,' he said. 'Concentrate on one constituency.' I followed his advice, and for the sake of convenience chose my own, Brent East, which at the time was one of the most ethnically and economically diverse constituencies in the country. The result of my efforts was *Across the Divide*. In light of my later plays, this appears quite primitive and clunky, lacking structure and narrative, but from the foothills of the post-Blair era, it is an intriguing social document.

As I worked on the script with the play's director Dominic Cooke and Graham Whybrow, literary manager at the Royal Court, I began to understand how to edit and juxtapose material in order to create debate and narrative. I maintain that it is just as important for the audience at a verbatim play to want to know what happens next as it is in any other play. No matter how compelling the speeches are in terms of truthfulness and revelation in their own right, the verbatim play must be more than a random collection of monologues if it is to sustain interest over a whole evening. A presentation of opposing viewpoints would be a turn-off in the same way. Just before my trip to Israel to research *The Arab-Israeli Cookbook*, the subject of the Israeli-Palestinian conflict was debated on *The Moral Maze* on Radio 4. Within seconds of each guest starting to talk, the debate degenerated into an exchange of accusations: 'We only did this because you did that'; 'Yes, but that's only because you had already done this, killed them, blown up that...' Can you imagine how dull it would be to have two hours of that on stage?

The underlying structure may not be as obvious as in a farce or a revenge tragedy, but a verbatim play should still be built around a narrative, and it must still set up dramatic conflicts and attempt to resolve them. Characters should be shown to undertake journeys of discovery of some kind, even if these journeys take place while the character is sat in a chair, talking. In my own plays I have moved from plays that comprise a succession of monologues, to something much more complex and intricately structured, weaving strands of narrative into the source material to give it shape and make it accessible and interesting. These narratives may take many forms – historical, emotional, psychological, or any combination of these. One example: when researching *Talking to Terrorists*, I interviewed people connected with the 1984 Brighton hotel bombing. After conducting separate interviews with Pat Magee, who planted the bomb in the Grand Hotel, and a woman who had been in the hotel at the time and was a victim of his actions, I intercut their monologues in the final script. As the characters' speeches alternated on stage, they acquired an irony and power neither would have had in isolation.

Across the Divide was given a reading at the Duke of York's Theatre, and in my first experience as a dramatist I sat and listened, finding it by turns marvellous and dreadful. More crucially, it was my good fortune that Max Stafford-Clark later read the script. Max had directed me in several plays by this time, and he is undoubtedly for actors, writers and directors alike one of the most influential and creative figures in recent theatrical history. He sent me a postcard reading, 'I've always liked this sort of project, but I found this particularly insightful and entertaining.' A full two years later he invited me out to supper and said, 'I don't know if you know, but I'm reviving *Rita, Sue and Bob Too* by Andrea Dunbar.' I assumed the next question would be 'Would you like to play the drunken father?', but Max continued: 'If you recall, it's set on the Buttershaw estate in Bradford, and I'm going to do it in conjunction with a new devised play about what's happened to the estate in the eighteen years since Andrea wrote her play. We would very much like you to write it.'

The play, *A State Affair*, opened at the Everyman Liverpool, and on the first night a record number of people walked out. Max was jotting them down in his notebook and told me afterwards in what order they left: 'There was a two, then two singles, then a three, then four all at once, then two more twos…' and so on. I convinced myself I had spawned a theatrical turkey, marking the end of my brief flirtation with the verbatim genre. Now, with the clarity of distance, I can attribute the mass exodus to another factor. Since Alan Clarke's film adaptation, *Rita, Sue and Bob Too* has been seen as an enjoyable sex romp. However, the original stage version is anything but, and the end of the play is as bleak as anything in modern drama. Our Liverpool audience were disappointed, and probably hoped that my play would deliver the light-hearted thrills they had expected. When this turned out to be just as bleak – and, what's more, drawn from real life – they decided to go…in their droves.

Perhaps what I am describing is an audience encountering an unfamiliar theatrical form and reacting to it in a confused or angry manner. Certainly there are other instances of such behaviour through theatrical history. In any case, as the playwright, I was feeling mortified. It was Sally Rogers, who played Natalie, who said to me afterwards,

'Did you see them?'

'Did I see who?'

'The audience.'

'Most of them seemed to leave.'

'A few of them…but didn't you see the ones who stayed…they were cheering and clapping with their hands above their heads, and some were in tears. I've not seen that for a long time. By the way, there are some people in the foyer who want to see you.'

I went to the front of the Everyman, and there by the entrance were four men. One of them shook my hand.

'Are you Robin?'

'Yes.'

'We just wanted to say thanks. We all sell the *Big Issue*. We know these people. We know some of the people in your play, and you've got them absolutely, and what they have to live through. You're the first person who's ever told it like it is... Good on you, mate, it was just brilliant.'

A State Affair went on two national tours, had two runs at the Soho Theatre, was recorded for Radio 3, and was eventually performed before an invited audience in the River Room at the House of Lords. When the words of those people – people whose voices would never normally be heard in the theatre – resounded around the grand cornices and vast paintings of naval battles at the epicentre of power, I felt I had been part of something really worthwhile.

•

A journalist once told me that her editor, having already written his story, told her to 'Go out and find someone to say *such and such*'. With a fixed agenda like this, all a writer can do is fill in the gaps. When I work on a project, I may bring along my own preconceptions, but I try not to anticipate what I'm going to find before I get there. If in my working methods I remain open and flexible, and explore as many avenues as possible, I give myself, and ultimately the audience, a better chance of discovering something new, and of having my expectations confounded. In Bradford, the research team all expected the world of heroin addiction to be grim. None of us was prepared for the vigour and commitment of the charismatic figures spawned by the crisis but determined to counteract it.

Discovering unexpected tellers of stories, 'mines' of information and interest, is an occupational hazard – or rather a recurring thrill – of verbatim research. I have sometimes worked with a small team of researchers to help me find people to talk to, sometimes with the other members of the theatre company, and sometimes in isolation. When conducting interviews for *A State Affair* in Leeds and Bradford, I worked with a team of actors. The advantage of this is that you can cover a lot of ground quickly, and in this case we had set up a lot of contacts in advance. We would meet at ten in the morning and depart in small groups to talk to policemen, primary school teachers, drug addicts, prostitutes, parish priests, prisoners…anyone who might have an insight into the problems we were investigating. In the course of our day's work, we might meet people tangentially: 'Oh, while you're here you ought to meet my sister', or 'We've got another inmate who's got a good story'. When I was researching *The Arab-Israeli Cookbook* I went to a winery in the desert to meet the owners, Arnon and Aheron. The conversation was hijacked by another guest, an extremely articulate and entertaining American woman called Rena. I asked her if I could come and see her two days later at her flat in Jerusalem. She said she would be delighted, and promptly became one of the protagonists of the play.

I am often struck by the fact that when subjects such as the Israel-Palestine conflict are debated, they remain the province of politicians, experts, professors and academics. Conversely, the people who are hardly ever asked for their opinion are the people who have to live with the situation day after day – in the case of *The Arab-Israeli Cookbook*, a hairdresser in an Arab village, a student working in a shopping mall to earn his tuition fees, a gay couple in Tel Aviv, a priest's wife in Bethlehem, a felafel maker in Jerusalem, a houmus maker near the wall. These are the people whose lives are most affected by the conflict, and yet they have traditionally been the least consulted. Surely, if we want real insight into any situation, we shouldn't listen only to those with an academic overview.

The level of insight available from unusual sources was powerfully demonstrated to me during the research for *A State Affair*. We would meet up as a company, and Max Stafford-Clark would ask, 'Who met anyone interesting?' Actors would report back, usually in the form of an improvisation in which they impersonated the interviewee, recreating the scene in which they were involved. If I thought this person's story might be incorporated, or if the actor said they were a character they'd like to play, we would go back and conduct more in-depth interviews.

At one of these workshops, Matt Wait, a very gifted actor, said he had come across a man called Paul, who had interested him greatly, but was very difficult to talk to because he was in such an advanced state of heroin addiction. 'White as a sheet,' Matt said, 'and dripping with sweat.' He poured a bottle of mineral water over his head to give us a better idea of what Paul looked like. Every time Matt had tried to talk to him, Paul had been either so drugged or so painfully turkeying that he was more or less incoherent.

One night we were waiting outside the crypt of the church where the homeless could get a corned beef sandwich and a cup of tea, when Paul came out. This was a rare occasion when he was clear-headed. Matt and I asked him to the pub, and he talked for three hours about his life. Here was a man who defied every notion of respectability, who would never be asked on to *The Moral Maze* or *Question Time*, or to partake in any think tank on the problems of drug abuse, and yet he had an absolute understanding of how he and others like him had come to be where they were, and what his prospects were. Politicians speak with apparently great authority on matters of urban deprivation, drug misuse and anti-social behaviour, yet I have never heard a politician speak about this kind of situation with anything like the perspicacity that Paul displayed that evening.

When we performed the play at the House of Lords, Paul's words made the audience gasp. I wouldn't say that verbatim theatre gives Paul a voice – he has a voice already – but it does provide his voice with listening ears: mine when he tells me his story, and those of the audience when the actor tells it to them. To provide a setting, the stage, where his voice can be heard is to provide an amplification of an otherwise lost voice – and is the reason why I think verbatim theatre is so important.

It's not just that so much of what comes out of the political arena is now warped and misrepresented, so that lives are reduced to statistics exchanged in the House of Commons. It's also that this 'official version' is the only account on offer. The verbatim playwright contends that the situation is more complex; that individuals should be allowed to speak for themselves. This is literally what verbatim theatre does: it allows people to speak for themselves. We are never going to crawl our way towards redemption and an understanding of the human condition if we listen solely to those looking to protect their own interests. Paul, like the Ancient Mariner, had no other agenda than to make me rise the morrow morn a sadder yet a wiser man.

The opposite of Paul was a young man I interviewed from the Israeli Embassy during the research for *Talking to Terrorists*. He did nothing more than trot out the official line, learnt by rote from the Embassy handbook. I knew no more at the end of the interview about him or the situation than I did at the beginning. People say to me, 'Isn't there something interesting in seeing him kowtow to the official version?' I can only say it's a matter of judgement. To me, what he said wasn't new; it wasn't honest, it wasn't personal, it wasn't anchored in personal experience. He saw me as an opportunity to distribute propaganda to a wider audience, and I resisted him. Some people are boring in a fascinating or amusing way, and others are just boring. And if it's boring, it renders the whole exercise futile. What's the point of gathering three hundred people in a darkened space merely to tell them something they've heard before, or worse, to send them to sleep?

This raises the question: 'What makes one person interesting and another dull?' For me, someone is interesting if they widen our knowledge of the complexity of the human condition, and bring fresh insight into the situation we're exploring. A character's dogmatism may be interesting as an example of bigotry prevailing in a certain context or circumstance, but it won't sustain an evening's exploration. However, I'm sure, given the same source material, different playwrights would make different choices, and this is why verbatim theatre is as creative a medium as any other.

•

For any playwright, there is a moment when what I would call the 'vision' of the play is revealed. The tone is established, the themes and the story coalesce and, most importantly, the shape of the drama becomes clear. At this moment it is the prerogative of the playwright, verbatim or otherwise, to choose the parts of the material which embody that vision most clearly. For the 'creative' playwright, this might happen in the depths of imaginative contemplation, before a word of dialogue is committed to the page. For the verbatim writer this process occurs in the editing, somewhere among the scraps of collected material strewn across the desk, as a unifying premise draws the various strands and stories together.

In my case, I have several notebooks and sheaves of paper covered with speeches and conversations. When collecting material, I favour a notebook and pen because they seem unthreatening; electronic gadgetry in the room doesn't tend to put people at ease. As a way into this mass of fascinating but disordered raw material, I use different coloured marker pens to underline passages with common themes, and to indicate what would be effective next to what. I always look for thematic links, allowing me to create a kind of relay race, with actors passing the baton on to each other. This helps with the narrative structure, but also raises the question of how much I'm manipulating my subjects and the stories they have told me, to fit them into a scheme of my own.

The accusation of manipulation is one of the principal objections to verbatim theatre. Just because I write about real people and seek to portray them honestly, is there an embargo on editing creatively? Would you say to photographers that they have no right to interpret – or to crop? That all their subjects should be filmed straight on, in nothing other than a flat light? To declare that, because subjects are real, they have to be portrayed in a way that fictional characters are not, is to undermine the power of the verbatim playwright. It prevents the tailoring of the material to make it political, emotional or even theatrical.

How is this creative editing any different from the spin that governments put on their material? I can only say that, unlike governments that edit in order to obfuscate and deflect attention, and therefore to limit our knowledge, I attempt to edit in order to enlighten and intrigue, and therefore to broaden our knowledge. If I create a dramatic ambiguity early in the play, which you might see at the time as limiting knowledge or sowing a seed of confusion, I only do so in order to engage the audience's natural inquisitiveness until a later moment, when I will clarify the point, and to make the clarification more emphatic because of the dramatic tension that has led to, and built up, that subsequent revelation.

This is what artists do: they try to broaden our knowledge –
knowledge of the world and self-knowledge. I would maintain
that the verbatim writer is as much an artist as a conventional
playwright. You would not say that a portrait painter who has a
subject sitting in front of them is less of an artist than a painter
who makes up a face from their imagination.

A second complaint about verbatim theatre is that it is
exploitative. I am often asked if my interviewees talk to me
willingly. I was in a bail hostel in Leeds interviewing two young
women about their lives of drugs and shoplifting and their
relationships. The sub-warden of the hostel suspected that I was
a cynical southern intellectual peddling northern angst and using
these girls' stories to make money or gain some kudos among the
intelligentsia. 'Never forget it's someone's life,' he said to me. I
don't believe I was guilty of any of these suspicions, but I have
been aware ever since of the potential for titillating an audience
at someone's expense. His warning echoes through all my work:
'Never forget it's someone's life.'

This became a central concern in my recent play *Life After
Scandal* – in effect a play about this very issue. Because the
subject of the play was the invasion of privacy, often accompanied
by vilification and in some cases misrepresentation, almost all
of my interviewees were discussing quite humiliating episodes
which had already been lived out in the public arena. The
dredging up of old traumas was painful for many of them, and
five of my interviewees asked for the right to veto the inclusion
of material in the final script. This gave them the safety net of
later retracting something they told me if they regretted saying it
or were worried about its meaning in a different context. For the

first time in my career, and because of the delicacy of the subject, I agreed to this request.

You could argue that after their various experiences at the hands of the British press, the *Scandal* interviewees were by now well practised in their dealings with media figures, and they probably saw my play as an opportunity to offer their version of events. But what about the 'everyday' people who have populated my other plays? Do they really know what they're letting themselves in for? I think they do know, and I think they value the chance to relate their account. When I was researching *A State Affair*, a young mother on a housing estate said to me:

'Are you really interested in talking to me?'

'Yes.'

'What...my whole life story?'

'Yes.'

'What...from the beginning?'

'Yes.'

'Really?'

'Yes.'

We sat down to talk at 4:15 in the afternoon, and she finished her narrative at 11:20 at night. As I left, she said, 'Thank you. I can't tell you how good I feel. I've never told my story before, not all of it like that. You made me feel it was important; that I am important. That's worth everything in the world to me.'

•

The process of conducting an interview can be roughly divided into three sections. First come the initial pleasantries on both sides:

'Do come in. Did you find us alright?'

'Yes, very good instructions, thank you. What a lovely garden.'

'Yes…south-facing, you know.'

'That's a nice photograph.'

'Yes, it's my sister Deidre and her husband on holiday in Corfu. Have a shortbread biscuit.'

Sometimes these pleasantries will be accompanied by domestic activity: children, dogs, cats, caged birds; cooking, laundry. When we arrived at Mo Mowlam's house during our research for *Talking to Terrorists*, Marjory the cleaner was vacuuming the living room carpet, because their Labrador puppy had chewed the ice tray for the fridge into small plastic shards.

Then comes the formal part of the proceedings. Everyone settles down and there is an interchange of views, and the telling of stories. I, or whoever is with me, will ask questions until there is a consensus that enough has been said.

The closing formalities tie things up:

'Sure I can't tempt you to another cup of coffee? What time's your train…well you should have plenty of time. Who else have you been talking to? Would you like a pot of Melanie's marrow chutney?'

It is surprising how much of my final material – you might even think a disproportionate amount – comes from sections one and three. But not so surprising when you think of what the theatre is about. Even from the main body of the interview I will select the material that is idiosyncratic, personal and emotional. The incidental domestic details which dovetail an interview are important because they humanise the situation. They are the common link between the interviewee and the audience; they make the audience care. When I put these dramas together, I'm not writing a thesis, I'm writing a play. And, unashamedly, I want the audience to care.

My need for specificity is the reason why I interrupt my interviewees in full flow only to ask for more detail. Natalie is sitting in her living room on the Buttershaw Estate in Bradford telling me her life story. She says at one point,

'I started to drink.'

Well, that's reasonably interesting, but I want more. Without looking up I ask,

'What? What were you drinking?'

'Abbey Royal…it's like a fortified wine, like a sherry…two pounds forty-five a bottle. I still drink it now…sometimes half a bottle, sometimes a whole bottle.'

That's not just interesting; it's poetic, moving, sad and funny at the same time – and riveting. On another occasion, Fatthiyah in the D'Heisheh Camp in Beit Jala is telling me about the day her third son Jad was killed:

'What was the weather like?'

'The days before had been cold, but that day was warm.'

'What was his last meal?'

'Stuffed zucchini and yogurt…he ate a small portion and then left the house hurriedly.'

'What was he wearing?'

'He was wearing a black T-shirt, and because the day was warm his face was glowing.'

I cannot recall these episodes, even now long after the events, without being moved. And of course, I also want my audience to be moved. If you look at any of the great playwrights – Shakespeare, Chekhov, Miller – it is the human detail which hooks an audience. Great drama gives playgoers a heightened emotional experience when strong narrative combines with the empathy that comes from recognition. A kind of enlightenment results. This is my aim: to use people's real words to move us to a new understanding of ourselves.

•

But do I ever cheat? Is there ever a tension between being truthful to the interviewees and creating something that I know is going to work theatrically? The answer is yes – but not a lot.

To expand on this admission, I would say that it depends on what is meant by being truthful: literal truth or truth in spirit? A literal truth would rely on an exact replication of the research in its entirety – a tiresome and practically impossible undertaking. My sense of 'truthfulness' to the interviewee puts the emphasis on representing them truthfully in spirit. I might make small changes to the text for the sake of clarity or fluidity, but I take great pains to preserve the sense, tone and thrust of an interviewee's words. If, for the sake of an *and* or a *but*, what they say becomes much clearer, I have no qualms about inserting such a word. Why alienate or confuse an audience for the sake of a monosyllable or two?

As for all the *ums* and *ers*, the stutters and repetitions, I use them when they suit my purpose, and leave them out when they don't. This is only another form of editing. If one of my interviewees becomes very emotional, I can retain all the verbal inconsistencies to highlight that. But if they're telling a story and I want the narrative to trot on at a good pace, I'll pare their words down to what is necessary. I can't include everything that I'm told by my subjects, so I must choose what I think is the most representative sample. For *Life After Scandal*, Jonathan Aitken told me five stories about his time in prison. To include all five would have been counter-productive; it would have thrown the play out of kilter. So I chose what I considered to be the best three, and hoped that I had walked the fine line between honouring the subject's integrity and serving the audience's interest.

Perhaps more controversially, if I interview two people and there's only room for one of them in the play, I feel justified in creating a composite character incorporating lines from both originals. This would not work if the characters were well-known public figures, of course; it would amount to putting words into their mouths. But for unknown characters who, in terms of the play, represent a certain circumstance or dilemma, this can be dramatically economic without becoming a misrepresentation.

Such judgement calls are part of my craft. I do what I think necessary to give my interviewees a fair hearing while providing the audience with a stimulating evening. Walking the line between the two is my dilemma. The need to entertain – and I do think verbatim plays should be entertaining – pulls me one way; the need to represent true life accurately pulls the other. In the end I believe I can be trusted to find the right balance. What do I base this claim on? Aside from my experience, I would put it down to a sympathetic nature – specifically a sympathy for both the subjects and the audience, at the same time.

•

I see a bright and varied future for verbatim theatre. It is my
intention to maintain a degree of flexibility in this work. I have
to some extent been responsible for the flourishing of the form,
but success brings innovation, and fresh approaches are now
springing up. This is exciting: no genre should become static
or formulaic. I've hinted already at a certain reluctance to
conform, and I certainly don't want to find myself hamstrung
by notions of my own making. The British love rules: 'These are
the rules for verbatim theatre.' I would resist any such notion
wherever possible.

•

Following the sentencing of Tony Martin, the Norfolk farmer who
shot two intruders in 1999, one of them fatally, the *Sunday Times*
of 30 April 2000 invited correspondence on the matter. A Justice
of the Peace from Somerset wrote:

'There is usually a whole battery of skilled and assiduous
apologists for these offenders. Every conceivable factor is
blamed for their offending, except their own weakness, cupidity,
immorality, fecklessness, and sheer malevolence.'

This has been the single most influential quotation on my journey
as a writer. I hope I am skilled. I think I am assiduous. And I am
an apologist and proud of it.

If there is one thing I have tried to nurture in my plays, it is the idea of the degree to which we are all vulnerable. 'There but for the grace of God go you or I.'

DAVID HARE &

MAX STAFFORD-CLARK

David Hare is an internationally performed playwright who has had thirteen of his plays produced at Britain's National Theatre, and ten presented on Broadway. In 1998, he performed his one-man play *Via Dolorosa*, a meditation on his journey through Israel and the Palestinian territory, in London's West End, transferring the following year to Broadway. In 2004, his play *The Permanent Way*, an investigation into the privatisation of the British railways, was premiered at the National Theatre, directed by Max Stafford-Clark. Later that year, his account of the events leading up to the Iraq War, *Stuff Happens*, a play which intersperses fictional scenes with occasional real-life direct address, also premiered at the National Theatre.

Max Stafford-Clark founded Joint Stock theatre company with David Hare, William Gaskill and David Aukin in 1975. *Yesterday's News* (1976) was the first Joint Stock play to use verbatim techniques. From 1979 to 1993 Max Stafford-Clark was Artistic Director of the Royal Court theatre. Here he continued to use research as an essential part of play-making and *Falkland Sound* (1983) is perhaps the most memorable verbatim play of his tenure at the Court. In 1993 he founded Out of Joint, which has produced three dramas using verbatim techniques in recent years: *A State Affair* (2000) and *Talking to Terrorists* (2005) by Robin Soans and *The Permanent Way* (2003) by David Hare.

(The following interview was conducted by Will Hammond on 19/04/07. Also present was Naomi Jones, Assistant Director of Out of Joint Theatre Company.)

HAMMOND

When did you first encounter verbatim theatre and what attracted you to it?

STAFFORD-CLARK

I first encountered verbatim theatre in 1976, with Joint Stock's third project *Yesterday's News*. We had embarked on a play that was to be written by Jeremy Seabrook, but after a bit it became clear that his analysis of society and Bill Gaskill's [co-founder of Joint Stock] were totally divergent and that a play wasn't going to come out of this particular voyage. So we abandoned ship, and Bill said, 'Well, let's do a verbatim play.' None of us had a clue what that meant. But we scoured the newspapers looking for material, and David Rintoul, who was an actor in the company, found this press clipping about the mercenary who shot his own people in Angola,* and Bill said, 'Well, let's do a story about that.' So for the next three weeks, all of us acted like journalists. Paul Kember, who was one of the actors, had been a journalist on the *Liverpool Echo*, and he got through to this guy who all the newspapers had been trying to get hold of, who had been recruiting these mercenaries, and who was perfectly willing to talk to us. And then through another actor, who had talked to a

---

* Costas Georgiou, aka 'Colonel Callan', executed 10 July 1976 for mercenary activity, including the murder of fourteen of his own men.

taxi driver, we met two of the mercenaries who had actually been there. And that was extraordinary.

We were rehearsing in this freezing room in St Gabriel's Parish Hall on the Churchill Estate in Pimlico, and David and I went to meet one of these guys in a local pub. He said, 'How much money have you got?' He thought we were a television company. So we said, 'A tenner', and he said, 'Well, I'll think about it, I may come, I may not.' So we went back to the other actors in this freezing cold rehearsal room and said, 'He may come or he may not, we've no idea', and suddenly the rehearsal room door burst open. He'd not used his hand, he'd actually kicked it open with his foot. And there were two of them. He'd phoned his mate. One of them came and stood right in the middle of the group, and the other one went round kicking open all the doors, so this freezing rehearsal room became even more freezing. And then the one who'd done all the kicking came back and said, 'So. You want to talk.' And they sat down, and they talked for three hours about being a soldier. Well we used it, of course.

One had been a para and one had been in the SAS. And one of them came from Walthamstow. Will Knightley, who was in the group, also came from Walthamstow, so the two of them bonded on a Walthamstow-level, like, 'Did you go to the Odeon on Sunday mornings?' – 'Yeah', and so on. And they talked about the best way of laying an electronic ambush in order to kill the most number of people, and they talked about it like a wine connoisseur would discuss different years of wine. And they were fascinating, really good raconteurs and absolutely racist. One of them talked about torturing in Northern Ireland: how they'd take 'Paddy' up in a chopper, take off his blindfold at 400 feet up, show him how high he was, then put the blindfold back on and come down to two feet off the ground and push him out. And one of them said, 'Those Irish bastards, I'd like to push Paddy out just when Mrs Paddy's hanging up her washing so he lands, splat, right in front of her.' It became the centrepiece of *Yesterday's News*.

Well, we knew we had a show then. We found the recruiter, a schoolgirl who'd had a pash on one of the boys who'd been sent out there, and another journalist, who'd covered the story. Once we'd spoken to them, the story came together remarkably quickly. And that's, in a way, what I've found about verbatim work: it takes quite a long time to find the story within the subject, but once you've found it things move remarkably quickly. We had a conventional rehearsal period, which I suppose must have been five weeks, but we probably only needed three. That was the first acquaintance I had with verbatim theatre. But Bill had had confidence about it as a way of working because he had used it for a play at the Royal Court called *Eleven Men Dead at Hola Camp*.

HARE

In the fifties, before the Theatre Upstairs was built, there were those Royal Court Sunday nights. The idea was that you would spend two weeks rehearsing something that was performed only once, and all sorts of very creative work followed. And people *in* the theatre would go to the Royal Court on a Sunday night, because if you were working in the theatre, and a professional, on your night off you could go to a play on the Sunday – because there was at that time very little fringe theatre as it's now understood. I think probably more than one documentary play was put on at the Royal Court at that time.

STAFFORD-CLARK

Well that was certainly the first one, *Eleven Men Dead at Hola Camp*.

HAMMOND

Did you subsequently use the verbatim technique in development work, even if you weren't necessarily going to create a verbatim play?

STAFFORD-CLARK

I've always used research. If you had a play with, let's say, a foreign correspondent in it or a schoolteacher, I would encourage the actors to talk to foreign correspondents or schoolteachers. Extensive research was always part of Joint Stock's repertoire. I can't say we talked to Chinese peasants for *Fanshen* because there weren't any immediately available, but certainly we researched the book as extensively as we could. During the workshop for *Serious Money*, by Caryl Churchill, it is true that we spoke to people and two actors got jobs on the floor of the futures exchange, but the product wasn't verbatim at all. A semi-verbatim project would be *Mad Forest*, also by Caryl Churchill, which was a perfectly realised play, but in the centre was a twenty-minute section which was the result of research that she and students from Central School of Drama gathered by visiting and talking to people in Romania. So that's a kind of hybrid. But yes, with *Serious Money*, there was no intention of making it a verbatim play, yet we did extensive research talking to people who worked in the city at all different levels.

HAMMOND

So verbatim is a research tool in that respect?

STAFFORD-CLARK

I'd say it's become so, yes. I mean really what a verbatim play does is flash your research nakedly. It's like cooking a meal but the meat is left raw, like a steak tartar. It's like you're flashing the research without turning it into a play. The hard thing is to turn it into dialogue, to make the transition between somebody talking to the audience and drama.

HARE

There's a very interesting passage that I used in *Via Dolorosa* which unfortunately got cut, where, in a book, George Steiner talks about what he regards as the Jewish genius. He says the Jewish genius is scientific not imaginative. The Jews, he claims, are essentially scientists. Their skill, their expertise, is for finding out about the world, and they're rather distrustful of the imagination because they don't see the need to invent stories or to make things up, because the world itself is so fascinating that all you need to do is investigate it. Now I'm not saying it's true, and blatantly there are so many great Jewish writers that at one level the theory is nonsense. But I understand and sympathise with the idea that the world itself is so interesting, why on earth would you want to add a layer on top of it, which is, as it were, only your own interpretation? Only a very great playwright would invent that soldier's line 'So. You want to talk', whereas the soldier has said it effortlessly. All the time you're coming across lines that are almost impossible to invent. In a way, all documentary plays are essentially saying the same thing, which is that the world is much more interesting than you think it is, people are much stranger than you think they are, the world is much more various, the way people look at the world is much wilder and much more unexpected. That's always the sign of a good documentary play: unexpectedness. The boring documentary plays are the ones that go over a field that you already know and you think, 'Oh yeah, well, they're soldiers, of course they think like soldiers.' But good documentary plays take you aback with, 'Oh my goodness, is that what they feel?'

STAFFORD-CLARK

There was one extraordinary moment in the second verbatim play I did, which was *Falkland Sound** at the Royal Court in 1983, exactly a year after the Falklands war. This woman who's a schoolteacher in the Falklands, and who'd been brought up in Liverpool and had been a Labour supporter all her life, recounted her conversion to being a Social Democrat. And it was because she had hosted a number of people on a particular Labour supporters' march that had come through Congleton in Cheshire, where she lived, and she'd said she would give them lunch. But none of them stayed to do the washing up. And then she said, 'I really fancied that David Owen a bit', and so that was her conversion to the SDP.† It changed her life absolutely.

HAMMOND

In terms of your writer-director relationship, is it different working on a verbatim play together than it is working on a fully imagined play?

* by Louise Page
† David Owen, Leader of the Social Democratic Party (SDP), 1983–7 & 1988–90

STAFFORD-CLARK

I'd say no, no difference.

HAMMOND

Would it be possible to make a verbatim play without a writer present?

STAFFORD-CLARK

No, impossible.

HARE

In *Taking Stock** Max describes a later period in Joint Stock's history in which the relationship between the actors and the writer became confused. The actors fell upon certain texts and felt that they were meant to pull them apart like wolves. There was a period where democracy of process was confused with democracy of function: everyone thought they had the right to write.

With *Fanshen*, Bill Gaskill and Max made a wonderful decision, which was that they would never go upstairs with me and bitch about the actors, that there would not be that separation, which happens on every play, where you stand there and say, 'Oh, she's not very good tonight, have you spoken to her?' And we banned those conversations, we simply said that the only forum in which we will discuss is a group forum. Wonderful. And what I call the 'fourth floor' approach to theatre – which is at the National Theatre where everybody who runs the theatre is on the fourth

* *Taking Stock: The Theatre of Max Stafford-Clark* by Max Stafford-Clark and Philip Roberts (London: Nick Hern Books, 2007)

floor and all the actors work downstairs, and then up come the directors and say, 'Oh my God, so-and-so's impossible. Oh, I can't stand working with so-and-so' – the 'fourth floor' approach was banned.

STAFFORD-CLARK

The first time I worked in New York I was working for the Hal Prince Organisation, and I did a run-through in front of the two producers, Hal Prince and his associate, and there was a very good actress in it who was having a very heavy period, and she said, 'Do you mind if I take it easy this morning?' and I said, 'No, not at all.' And afterwards the two producers said, 'You want to fire her, we can get someone else in by Monday.'

HARE

Exactly. So what Max and Bill did very brilliantly on *Fanshen* was remove the idea that the director was the only judge, the arbiter. You had to work with the actors, and if you wanted the play presented in a certain way, the only way you could do that was by arguing for it with the actors. But I think on subsequent productions the actors then became a little over-excited by this idea and started interrogating the text in a rather Stalinist way.

When we did *Fanshen* we were really finding our way. And we didn't know what the hell we were doing, because for better or worse it was a very radical way of presenting a play, and we groped our way to it. It was just chance that, the day before we started, either Max or Bill said, 'We're not going to discuss the actors except in their presence.' Because of the nature of the subject matter, group discussion became the means by which notes were given: not by Max and Bill but by self-criticism. It was very laborious, but the actor would say, 'I didn't think I was very good in scene seven because I missed such-and-such', and the group discussion would start. Whereas when I came to work with Max on *The Permanent Way*, the whole method had become a very lean machine.

HAMMOND

So the actors don't go through that same laborious self-criticising process?

STAFFORD-CLARK

Well that was a product of the political context of the work we were doing. No, they don't. But I think you do still give actors possession of the character they're playing.

HAMMOND

So given that the actors, as you say, take possession of their characters – in this case, their interviewees – does that mean the making of a verbatim play is in some sense more democratic?

STAFFORD-CLARK

Essentially yes, I think that the actors possessing the materials and feeling protective about the characters they're playing is an advantage if it's used right. I've never found that a disadvantage.

JONES

But equally that doesn't diminish the writer's role, does it?

STAFFORD-CLARK

Not at all. I think both Joint Stock and Out of Joint have sensed the correct moment to pass the material back to the writer.

HARE

Well, I think you learnt that, didn't you?

STAFFORD-CLARK

Yes.

HARE

By the time I arrived to do *The Permanent Way* Max was unbelievably sophisticated about the process simply because he'd been through it so many times.

STAFFORD-CLARK

I guess really what it is is a confidence that a play would emerge out of this period of research, the workshop with the actors and the writers.

HARE

Fanshen was, as we jokingly used to say, our *Mousetrap*: it was endlessly revived. And I was once left to rehearse it because Bill and Max weren't available. I thought I knew how to do it but it turned out I didn't have the slightest idea. I remember the rehearsal being absolutely humiliating. I thought I understood the process whereby it had been put together – I didn't at all. And the same thing happened with *Stuff Happens*. Max had an approach which involved actors re-enacting the real-life people they'd interviewed, with two actors sometimes playing the same person. But when I started a workshop with Nick Hytner,* who was unfamiliar with this method of workshop, I was essentially bringing my understanding of Max's method to bear on this

---

* Director of the premiere of *Stuff Happens*, 2004

material about the diplomatic process leading to the Iraq war. I discovered that I didn't understand the exercises at all, and that in my hands they were completely useless.

HAMMOND

What do you find useful during workshops?

HARE

To have as much presented to you as possible, and to be able to be supple, to be able to change the direction of the workshop at high speed. You've got to turn on a sixpence. You've got to say, 'We're wasting our time doing this, let's head off after that.' By the end of the *Stuff Happens* workshop, which came to life by chance, I was sending away dozens of people that we had been planning to interview. We were able to spin it around very quickly, and I think that's very important. You don't decide in advance which way it's going to go. As Eisenstein said, 'You must go where the film leads you.'

HAMMOND

At what point in the development of *The Permanent Way* did David become involved? Was it from the start?

STAFFORD-CLARK

Right from the start, yes. I approached him with this article in the *Guardian* that Ian Jack subsequently turned into a small book called *The Crash that Stopped Britain**. It was a kind of contemplation: he was sitting on the top deck of a bus stranded in a traffic jam on a railway bridge looking out over deserted, rusting

*   (London: Granta, 2001)

marshalling yards, pondering how what had once been the pride of the British Empire, our chief export, railways, which had tied India together, had become something so shameful.

HAMMOND

Unlike a play such as *Talking to Terrorists*, which is about our perception of a global, cultural phenomenon, behind *The Permanent Way* there is already a story of sorts to latch on to. Is there a distinction to be made between those two types of play in terms of the way that you go about making them?

STAFFORD-CLARK

No. David had to find the story within the story.

HARE

With *The Permanent Way* I had no interest in writing a play purely about the railways. In fact, I didn't know how to write it. But as soon as a woman arrived and talked about the difference between the attitude of the bereaved and the attitude of the survivors and the two different attitudes to grief – namely that the people who had survived wanted to accelerate away and put the event in the past, whereas the people who had lost their loved ones, their closest relatives or partners, wanted to go on investigating the incident and recriminate – and the subsequent war between those people – then the metaphor of the play, which is essentially about deciding what is necessary suffering and what is unnecessary suffering, immediately became a metaphor about human life itself. What larger question can you ask about life than 'What do we need to suffer and what do we not?' That's the most important argument human beings can have while they're here.

So, suddenly, this whacking great metaphor arrives, and it isn't a play about the railways.

A friend of mine from America came to see the play and said, 'Well I didn't think a play about the privatisation of the British railway system was going to be anything to do with me, but I'm a gay man in New York so of course for me it's about AIDS.' He's right. Same argument: could this have been prevented? That is the question the play is asking, and of course it's the overwhelming question about AIDS: how much of this had to happen and how much could have been prevented?

In this sense, there is absolutely no difference between the writing of a good documentary play and the writing of a wholly imagined play, because it's about the same thing, which is wanting to create something in the space between what the audience is feeling and what's going on on stage. What all playwrights address is the event between the stage and the audience, i.e. the unspoken stuff that's going on in the theatre. That's the point of theatre: there's a whole lot of unspoken stuff that's going on in the air.

And so you have to organise the material just as you organise the material as a playwright, to lead the audience in a certain way, through the material. And you have to have a metaphor. If the documentary play doesn't have a metaphor, just as if a purely imagined play doesn't have a metaphor or doesn't have a metaphorical element, then it's incredibly boring. It's a total misunderstanding of documentary theatre to think that it's all about just presenting a load of facts on the stage. You fight this vulgar misapprehension all the time.

STAFFORD-CLARK

Absolutely. Recently I've done two workshops about *The Permanent Way*, and at a distance of two years since we did it I see clearly that the structure and the skill with which we're sidestepped into the story are absolutely terrific. It's a very artful piece of writing.

HARE

It just happens to use lines that I've been given by other people.

HAMMOND

But you do take those lines and invest them with your own rhythms.

HARE

Yes. Empson: 'The careless ease always goes in last.'

STAFFORD-CLARK

Also we recontextualise them slightly.

HAMMOND

So is there ever a tension between being faithful to your interviewees and making a good drama?

STAFFORD-CLARK

Yes, and just like this interview, where you're going to choose and edit what is said, that's what you do. So some of the things we say in this interview you will cut for reasons of length or whatever. The only complaint we had about *The Permanent Way* was from Chris Garnett, the Chief Executive of GNER, who rang up to complain not that we had misquoted him, but that we had

omitted him saying pompously how many safety measures GNER
had put in place after a particular crash.

HARE

What happened was that I had not even attended the interview
with Chris Garnett. It had been done by actors and they gave
me the dialogue. Chris Garnett said – and it was a particularly
telling point – that when this fatal accident happened at Hatfield
he went to the scene of the crash thinking he'd be culpable as
the train operator. When he got there, a policeman said, 'It's all
right, it's not a problem with the operators, it's a broken rail. It's
a problem with the track.' And Garnett said, 'Thank Christ it's
not our crash.'

Now at the time he actually went on to say to the actors, 'Not
that I wasn't very upset about the crash. I was.' But I had not put
that in the play because I didn't know he'd said it. The actors
hadn't told me. But the minute he complained that he'd said
that, 'Right,' I said, 'I totally agree, I can see I'm misrepresenting
you, I'll put it in the play', and I put the line in. Now after this
happened he spoke to *The Times*, and *The Times* of London had
a full-page article called, 'Knight of long knife leaves blood on
tracks'. I must admit it did make me laugh. Here I am, being held
to account for one half-quotation based on a misunderstanding
which I immediately corrected. Does anyone seriously imagine
that journalists on Murdoch papers behave with anything like
the same understanding or alacrity? If journalists were held to
account for the truthfulness of the way they represent their
subject in interview, then *The Times* would be nothing except
apologies for what appears in *The Times*. In my experience

newspapers are a rich mix of what people never meant combined artfully with what people never said.

HAMMOND
Do you see verbatim as having a journalistic function?

HARE
It does what journalism fails to do.

STAFFORD-CLARK
All plays are a combination of journalism and autobiography, aren't they? If you write a play, let's say, about a difficult family or a failing marriage, then probably you draw on autobiography. If, on the other hand, you write a play about any subject that's remote from you, or if you're writing a play about a collapsing marriage but the principal character is, let's say, a foreign correspondent, then you want to do some research on that. So research and autobiography are the two shire horses that pull the writer's plough. I think that the theatre in this country has learnt more from journalism than it has from any other medium in the last twenty years.

HAMMOND
And do you think that explains the current interest in verbatim theatre?

HARE
No. The world is changing. Very, very complicated things are happening that people struggle to understand, and journalism is failing us, because it's not adequately representing or interpreting these things. Plainly, at a very simple level, British journalism

and American journalism misreported the great story of the time: many of them fell hook, line and sinker for the Blair/Bush propaganda during the years before the Iraq War. And the more august East Coast newspapers such as the *Washington Post* and *The New York Times* have actually published apologies. They have said on their front pages: 'We misrepresented this story, we didn't get it, we told it wrong.' So, obviously, journalism in America, less so in Britain, is in some sort of ethical crisis about how they came to be so complicit with the regime – 'What was the blackmail following 9/11 that made us incapable of doing the job of reporting?' Now the theatre rushes to fill that void because journalism isn't doing the job.

HAMMOND

In *Stuff Happens* you chose to use some speech that was real in the midst of your imagined dialogue. Do you make any distinction when placing them side by side?

HARE

I had a convention which was if somebody spoke directly to the audience it was on the record, stuff that I was replicating, but as soon as the doors closed and you went into a scene between characters, it's completely imagined. One of the problems with some documentary theatre is that it tends to lack scenes between people. It involves an awful lot of direct address. Clearly nobody knows what happened when Blair met Bush in Crawford, Texas, in April 2002 – and I mean nobody, they didn't even have assistants around them. These two men went for a walk in the woods. So it's left to me to imagine what happened between Blair and Bush, it's totally imagined. I'm very proud of the fact that nobody has ever said to me of *Stuff Happens*, 'I don't think it was quite like that', except in one specific area which I then changed for the New York production.

HAMMOND
What was that?

HARE
The degree to which Colin Powell was or wasn't complicit. I had taken an overly charitable view of Powell's behaviour, and when the play appeared in London a number of people who knew the events very closely and were at the centre of them said, 'You've been too kind to Powell.' In shorthand, I changed him from a liberal hero to a tragic hero. And it made a better play.

HAMMOND
A transformation seems to take place between interviewing someone in a personal conversation and them becoming a character in a drama. Is there a point in the process when you take ownership of those people and turn them into characters?

STAFFORD-CLARK
Yes, I think for the actors, who, after all, often commit themselves to the play before the play is written, it's important in the research to find a character they can possess and who they identify with. And it's true that in *The Permanent Way*, as in, I think, almost every other play I've worked on in this way, there were characters whom David hadn't actually met, or whom he met for the first time when we were performing, or in the bar after the play. So the actors feel a real possession and protectiveness about those characters, because their version of them is what's played.

HARE

But in *The Permanent Way*, I'd have to say that the actors were wonderfully accurate. When I subsequently met the people that they had presented to me, I wasn't surprised. The actors had been very faithful messengers.

HAMMOND

So if the actors have this possession of the character, how does that change your relation to them as the director?

STAFFORD-CLARK

Well, it's what you try to give actors all the time, so actually it's easier in this kind of work because they've met them. Naomi [Jones] and I did a workshop yesterday with this school in North London who are doing a production of *The Permanent Way*, and actually, although we played various games and did exercises that we had used during the original production, what was most useful for them was our account of the people we'd interviewed and what they were actually like, particularly the Squadron Leader.

You're not doing impersonations of these people, but you are trying to capture their spirit in some way. Quite a lot of rehearsal is working out how you define that. And it is very exciting when two actors return from an interview with a new character. Usually I get them to play the character simultaneously, so that the rest of the group becomes the interviewer and they both become the character, irrespective of sex. It often leads to quite fascinating moments when they respond simultaneously to a particular question. So even though we say it's not *Bremner, Bird and Fortune*, actually, observation and accuracy, which are part of any actor's training, are very much what you look for.

HAMMOND

There must be a lot of potential for humour.

STAFFORD-CLARK

Yes.

HAMMOND

Do you find yourselves restraining the comedy given that so much verbatim theatre is about deeply disturbing subjects?

STAFFORD-CLARK

No, I can't say we do. You look for the laughter and you look for the dialogue, and they're all helpful points along the way. But there are lessons. For example, in *The Permanent Way* the Bereaved Mother talked about the death of her son, and she talked about identifying him in the morgue. She said, 'They'd given him a parting and a fringe, and he'd never had a fringe in his life.' And if you just encountered those words on the page you'd think she was intending to horrify or chill the audience, whereas in fact she told it as a joke. Her 'action' was to entertain the audience with what was, to her, an amusing factor. So, in this instance, the humour provided a corrective to the assumption that because something is about death it must be chilling.

HAMMOND

You describe her action as being directed towards the audience rather than another character. Is that a distinctive quality of verbatim theatre?

STAFFORD-CLARK

It is, but it's also common to say Shakespeare or Restoration writers, where a good proportion of Restoration plays, often as much as a fifth, were in the form of asides to the audience. And the interesting thing is that in both Shakespeare and Restoration plays, characters always tell the truth to the audience, whereas they lie like fuck to each other.

HAMMOND

There are a couple of moments in *The Permanent Way* where a character addresses you personally.

HARE

Yes, I used the word 'David' deliberately to remind the audience that that's the context in which the whole thing's happening. There's that lovely moment in *Come Out Eli** when one of the characters actually propositions the author. It was terribly funny. I also did it in *Via Dolorosa* but essentially as a fake character.

HAMMOND

Why did you decide to perform *Via Dolorosa* yourself?

HARE

Because the metaphor of the play was not about Israel and the Palestinian territory, it was about the contrast between the lives of people in certain parts of the world for whom everything is effectively at stake in every daily decision, as opposed to those who live in the West who face no such daily pressure. So there had to be a character who represented somebody who has

* by Alecky Blythe. See pages 88–9.

nothing at stake, namely myself. The whole vitality of the play comes from the author visiting a place where where you live, what you eat, who your friend is, what street you're in, what club you belong to, what university you go to, where every decision you make is potentially life-changing, and arguments are not arguments like dinner-party arguments, they're arguments about whether you're going to survive or not, according to how you argue and what you come to believe. So I wanted to contrast that society, in which what you believe is tested at the most profound level, with the society in which I live, where I can pick up any opinion in the street, walk around and say 'I believe this', say 'I believe that', and I'm not going to be tested.

HAMMOND
So you became a character in that play?

HARE
Precisely. One of the things Stephen Daldry* kept saying to me was that you have to make yourself a character and you have to give yourself characteristics. And, in fact, having worked with Joan Didion on *The Year of Magical Thinking*, I think the reason that the producer wanted me to direct it originally, quite apart from the fact that Joan was seventy and had never written a play, was that it was a one-person show. Joan asked me, 'What is most difficult in the one-person show?' I said, 'Inventing your own character. You have to let go of who you really are and create a sort of fictional character.'

* Director of the premiere of *Via Dolorosa*, 1998

And it's true. You have to get yourself right, you have to decide who you are, and that may involve fictionalising yourself. So in *Via Dolorosa* I made myself stupider and more ignorant than I in fact was, because in fact when I went to Israel and the Palestinian territory I knew quite a lot. In reality, a lot of the exchanges were very equal, which is rather uninteresting, but as soon as I made myself stupid and ignorant –

STAFFORD-CLARK
An innocent hero.

HARE
Yes – then something much more interesting began to happen. Now similarly, Joan, in what you might say is a verbatim play – because a lot of what Joan is describing, in a play that is essentially about the death of her husband and the death of her daughter, are the things that her husband and daughter said – Joan had no scruples if I said, 'Look I need a moment at which you realised this or you realised that.' She'd say, 'Okay, I'll write you a moment.' And I got to a point where I couldn't remember what had actually happened and what we were saying had happened, because actually she was dramatising things that needed to be dramatised – and which were true – but which didn't necessarily happen in the events or in the order that she put them.

STAFFORD-CLARK
You also have to define who you're talking to. You have to, as it were, cast the audience. To give you an example, Sebastian Barry writes very lyrical, quite highly wrought plays in which characters justify themselves, so casting the audience is very

important. For example, in *The Steward of Christendom* there's a man whose death probably takes place ten seconds after the play ends, who's justifying his relationship with his daughters, the actions he's taken in his professional life, his marriage, to the audience, who are a kind of jury trying him, although they don't know that, obviously, when they come in, but he casts them as that. So, in the same way, *The Permanent Way*, like a number of other verbatim plays, casts the audience. And often, we cast the audience as us: the actors and creative team in the workshops. For example, the Police Superintendent: he wants to be thought of as being like a US marshal, riding into town, sorting out the trouble-makers, so his self-definition is that he's a hero. But who's he talking to? A bunch of actors. What does he think of a bunch of actors? Well, it's probably more interesting than talking to the Lions in Surbiton, but they probably don't know much about the railways. Although he might think, 'That one was in *The Bill*, I remember that one', and there's some sort of respect given to them, it's not on a professional level, more on a curiosity level really.

HARE
The thing is, people like talking to theatre people, and they trust them, and they talk much more freely to playwrights and directors and actors than they do to journalists.

STAFFORD-CLARK
I think that's absolutely true, they like their stories to be told. And they trust that their stories will be told.

HARE

We don't have the bad record journalism has for misrepresenting people.

HAMMOND

But you have the same power to misrepresent them.

HARE

Yes, but I've heard very few examples where people have gone to plays and felt misrepresented. I think it's to do with the act of standing up and pretending to be somebody, which I believe is a revelatory process, while just putting lines of writing down on a page is less revelatory. In other words, I believe print is much more manipulative than performance. I think the truth of what goes on is revealed in performance, whereas the truth of what goes on is not so clearly revealed by being written down on the page.

For example, in *Via Dolorosa*, the climactic encounter is with this great woman called Shulamit Aloni, who is a very volatile woman who shouts and screams and changes her mind all the time. My encounter with her was incredibly dramatic, so it became the climax of the play. And Shulamit's family and friends who came to see the play said, 'Shulamit, you've got to see yourself on stage. It's absolutely fantastic, it's on Broadway, the whole audience is roaring with laughter and they love you, and you're the big climactic character.' And Shulamit finally came to see the play and afterwards she was ashen, she was absolutely ashen, and she said to me, 'I had no idea how offensive and unpleasant I am.' And I said, 'Do you feel I've misrepresented you?' And she said, 'No, I'm so upset because I feel this is a true portrait of me.'

And she was horrified. And I said, 'But the audience loves you, everybody in the audience loves you', and she said, 'I know the audience loves me, but I don't love me.' It was awful.

STAFFORD-CLARK

Similarly, in *A State Affair* by Robin Soans,* there was a woman who ran a halfway hostel that was Christian, but she defined her own version of Christianity. And she was quite…racist, I think is probably the word, saying that Asians were universally the drug-dealers in the area, and that they were the people who should be weeded out. She didn't feel in the slightest bit ashamed about this. A liberal audience automatically clocked those views and adjusted themselves to absorb them, even though they knew that, as liberals, they didn't identify with them. But she didn't feel in the slightest bit reticent or ashamed about expressing those particular views at all.

HAMMOND

Given that there's this potential for exploitation, but there's also this sense of honour, which you've described, on the part of the theatre-maker, have you encountered verbatim theatre where you felt that that honour had not been upheld?

HARE

No. What you call verbatim – I don't know what verbatim theatre is – but what you call verbatim theatre raises moral questions. In *Via Dolorosa* I represented thirty-three people, and to most of them I sent their section of the play and I said, 'This is what I'm going to represent you saying, are you at peace with that?'

*   See pages 27–9

And I showed them what it was they were going to say. When they were people who I knew would disapprove of the way I represented them, I changed their names. But, in fact, when the settlers came to see *Via Dolorosa* they were more upset by the audience's reaction to them than by what I'd said. By definition Israeli settlers live among like-minded people. Suddenly they're in New York in a liberal Jewish audience and they're being laughed at for their views. They came backstage and one of the settlers said to me, 'You're a very, very brilliant propagandist, but that's what it is, it's propaganda.' And I said, 'But have I represented you accurately?' And she said, 'Yes, those are the things we said.' 'Well then,' I said. And she said, 'Yes, but they sound different when they're said on a stage in New York than when I said them at the time.' And I said, 'Well, is it possible that you're hearing them for the first time?' But I knew she would feel she had been manipulated simply because some of the things she had said were so horrifying – for example, her racist views about Arabs, which were so disturbing to me – and yet they were obviously the currency of how you spoke in the settlements on an everyday basis. And also the way they spoke about Rabin. She couldn't deny the things that had been said about Rabin: a group of settlers sat together and told me that Rabin had organised his own assassination. They said that, and they didn't deny they said that, but they knew that when it was said on the stage it didn't look good for them.

HAMMOND
So verbatim is a recontextualising process?

STAFFORD-CLARK
Yes.

HAMMOND

And rather than being any one thing, it inhabits a spectrum – a spectrum between reality and fiction?

HARE

Exactly.

STAFFORD-CLARK

I think what it is is an extra weapon that we've discovered, which liberates the writer occasionally from the word-processor in the garret or wherever they write these days; it's actually a resource they can place at their disposal. What they then do with it is as up to the writer as it ever was.

HARE

Look, I don't know what the genre is, in the sense that I saw the Tom Stoppard trilogy, *The Coast of Utopia*, in New York, which is an incredible achievement, but the second play I personally found profoundly offensive. There was a speech in it when Herzen* has just lost his child and he makes a speech in which he says that, well, we can't expect very much of human life. Human life is no more than the flowering of a lily, and it's almost arbitrary the moment at which a lily dies. So for a man to say that about the death of his child I found very offensive, and I said, 'My God, what is Tom saying here, I'm very shocked by this play, it seems to me an incredibly right-wing play.' I was very, very upset by it. Bob Crowley, who designed it, said to me, 'Actually he's quoting Herzen word for word. Tom had to put the speech in the play

---

* Alexander Herzen (1812–70), Russian writer and main character of *The Coast of Utopia*

because he felt if you don't hear Herzen's reaction to the death of his child, you have missed one of the most significant things in his life, however shocking it is.' So. It wasn't Tom, it was Herzen. I haven't seen anybody describe *The Coast of Utopia* as a verbatim play, but it is.

The overall thing I would say about this kind of theatre, which I've argued in *Obedience, Struggle and Revolt,** is that the objection to this sort of theatre is usually that it's not 'proper' and that it doesn't involve the degree of suffering that writing a play about your family would involve. But this is an objection to all political theatre or social theatre, or to use it in that Jewish sense, scientific theatre, theatre which seeks to describe the world – that it must somehow involve less emotional effort than a 'my mother didn't love me' play. And what I say in the essay is that I can't imagine that *The Life of Galileo* or *Mother Courage* cost Brecht any less than *Long Day's Journey into Night* cost O'Neill. We can see *Long Day's Journey into Night* cost O'Neill a great deal, it's written all over the play, but do you think Brecht writing about selling out and accommodation didn't cost him a lot? The idea that this kind of political, social, realistic theatre is less profound, this claim I find completely ridiculous.

*   (London: Faber and Faber, 2005)

ALECKY BLYTHE

Alecky Blythe's first play, *Come Out Eli*, was performed at the Arcola Theatre in 2003 and transferred to BAC as part of the Time Out Critics' Choice Season 2004. Following its unexpected success, Alecky founded her company Recorded Delivery to develop her unique approach to verbatim theatre. As Artistic Director, her productions include *All the Right People Come Here* (Wimbledon Studio), *The Day of All the Days* (Café Direct Flight 5065) and *Cruising* (Bush Theatre). Her other productions include *Strawberry Fields* (Pentabus), *I Only Came Here for Six Months*, a British Council commission (KVS Brussels) and *A Man in a Box*, written for the IWC Media/Channel 4 Coming Up Scheme. Her play *The Girlfriend Experience* will premiere at the Royal Court in September 2008.

I only ever wanted to be an actor, but a tour of *Frosty the Snowman* around supermarket forecourts was not the career I had in mind. Faced with ever more depressing prospects, I signed up for Mark Wing-Davey's course 'Drama Without Paper' at the Actors Centre in London, in the hope of creating my own work. My aim was to make a play that would showcase my talents as an actor, secure me an agent who could save me from the wilderness of Theatre in Education tours, and put me in the spotlight of television. As a result of Mark's inspirational workshop, I have now made a total of seven shows, and I currently have three more in the pipeline.

I wish I could lay claim to worthier intentions than simply getting a part in *The Bill*, but perhaps it was my naively self-interested approach that turned this first play into the success it was, far surpassing any bit-part on prime time television. In hindsight, having now made commissioned plays, I enjoyed incredible freedom during this early creative process. I was not hindered by the thought of literary managers and critics picking my work apart, which I consciously have to block out now. Really, I was just pleasing myself. As well as this, I was blissfully unaware of the verbatim 'genre' I was stepping into. Although I have always been a keen theatregoer, I would go to the theatre as a source of entertainment more than political debate, so I was wholly unaware of the other practitioners in the field, who tend to have a political focus. This ignorance saved me from trying to emulate a particular style or follow a set formula. If you haven't read the rules, it is much easier to break them.

Mark's approach was simple: find a good talking-point, interview a variety of people around the subject, and always be open to wherever the interview might lead. Mark had learnt the technique from the American actress Anna Deavere Smith, whose first ensemble show, *House Arrest*, he had directed in 1998. Anna would record interviews with people and then learn them word-for-word, appropriating the speaker's cadences and patterns of speech in very fine detail. She learnt the interviews by listening to them, phrase by phrase, through earphones, and then repeating each phrase exactly as it had been said, immediately after she had heard it. For her one-woman shows, in which she played multiple characters, she developed a method of performance that enabled her to morph from one character into another with superb vocal and physical dexterity. Audiences were amazed at her ability to transform. Crucially, her work demonstrated that language was the root of character. By copying their speech-patterns with such precision, the real person behind the performance shone through. What Mark noticed was that in rehearsals, while the earphones were still on, the delivery was all the more extraordinary. He decided to keep them on during the performance.

I have chosen to do this too, naming my company *Recorded Delivery* to reflect the performance style. It is true that not all actors have Anna's aptitude for learning and retaining a speech-pattern so accurately – the struggle to resist one's own natural rhythms is immense – but this is not the only reason for the method's success. In my experience, as you get further into a run, over-familiarity with the material actually deadens the performance. The fear of going on stage without knowing your lines certainly makes for very exciting theatre, but there is also something magical about the unique level of spontaneity that unlearnt delivery demands. As well as speaking, the actors are forced actively to listen to their lines. With so much going on in their heads, this leaves almost no time to consider how they will deliver them. The performances that result tend to be unselfconscious and incredibly free.

This always surprises actors new to the technique, as the idea of being fed a line sounds restrictive, but once actors have memorised their lines, they stop listening to how they were actually spoken in the first place, and this is when they start deviating from the original intonation and embellishing it. I have continued to work with earphones precisely to prevent this from happening. I do not deny that actors are highly skilled at interpreting their lines, but the way the real person said them will always be more interesting. My first outing into television confirmed this for me, when the use of earphones was ruled out.

I had suspected that convincing the producers to film actors with their earphones on was highly unlikely, but I assumed that the cast would at least be able to listen to the audio as an aid to rehearsal. To my dismay, even this was not allowed, and the actors worked instead from a transcribed text. In the event, they did a fine job, and the producers were happy with the outcome, but I had seen the text performed on stage with earphones, and the difference was substantial – much more interesting to listen to than the performances on screen. It is an actor's instinct to perform: to heighten, to try to make their lines 'more interesting' in an effort to project their character and make the person they are playing seem real. When you are recreating pre-recorded, everyday speech, this is not the best approach, because everyday speech is often more mundane and 'everyday' than anyone dares to invent. This is what gives it the ring of truth.

•

Audiences are often amazed at how willing people are to tell their stories. Because we do not listen to each other enough in daily life, when someone offers an attentive ear, people grab the opportunity to talk – even about highly personal information. You can gain access to many hidden worlds simply by giving a person the opportunity to speak. People are flattered that someone wants to listen, and in our celebrity-obsessed times, the idea of being a character in a play can be an exciting prospect. When I began working on one of my current projects, *The Girlfriend Experience*, which is about prostitution, I placed an advert on the internet. I was surprised at how quickly a group of women working in a parlour responded to it and took me into their confidence. Normally, the girls are very sceptical of any media interest in them. They are regularly approached by daytime chat shows, which persuade them to appear on the pretext of discussing 'Women in Business' or 'Empowered Women', only to reveal them to be prostitutes on live TV. In a similar way, some are concerned that my plays exploit their interviewees.

As it happens, I believe that these women see my play as a genuine opportunity to show the outside world a side of prostitution that is rarely seen. These women are not in the grip of drug addiction or pimps. With one exception, they are all assertive and mature, and they see themselves as independent businesswomen who are doing what they can to attain a better quality of life. They take pride in their work and the parlour. Its owner has freed herself from working for other, less favourable establishments, and having set the parlour up by herself, she has recruited the closest of her former colleagues to work alongside her. She is a woman 'doing it for herself', and she wants the world to know. The people I interview are not naive, innocent victims. In fact, one of the interviewees featured in another of my plays, *Cruising*, loved the play so much that they actually wrote to a reviewer, who had accused me of exploitation, in order to set the record straight.

The 'recorded delivery' technique has a further advantage, though. It allows interviewees to share highly personal information while offering a degree of protection for their identities. Maureen, the lead character in *Cruising*, actually appeared first as a minor character in an early version of *Strawberry Fields*. She was very disappointed when she ended up being cut from the final piece, so when I told her I wanted her to be the central figure in a new play, she was delighted. She made a fabulous main character. Not only did she enjoy talking, but she was extraordinarily frank, sometimes to the point of offending those around her. She was candid about all areas of her life, particularly her love life, on which the play focused. When a TV production company approached me with a view to making a documentary about her, Maureen tentatively agreed, and we filmed a ten-minute taster to pitch to channels. By the time the company had found a potential buyer for the film, though, Maureen had found a partner and was no longer willing to go public about her prolific dating past. Admittedly, her circumstances had changed, but by using only her words in the play, I had protected her identity, allowing her to speak freely, safe in the knowledge that she could walk down the street without being recognised. Cameras may present something closer to actual reality, but audio allows for greater access to underground worlds.

●

When I embark on a project, I never know where it will end up. The idea for the play is merely a starting-point, and you have to be open to wherever it may lead. The idea behind my first drama, *Come Out Eli*, was to make a play about fear. The Hackney Siege, which had begun on Boxing Day 2002, struck me as a good place to collect interviews about this subject. I couldn't have known when it began that the stand-off with gunman Eli Hall would end up lasting fifteen days, one of the longest sieges in Britain's recent history.

Come Out Eli established a formula that I used for *Strawberry Fields* and my other early plays. It was essentially about a community reacting to an event, and was fashioned from numerous interviews with a variety of people. I had walked right into the heart of a great story, so even though it was a series of intercut monologues, the unfolding of events during the siege provided a strong narrative arc. This wasn't always the case with the other plays. Nevertheless, it was easier to keep the audience entertained, because in these plays the actors were constantly changing from one character to another, partly in order to push the narrative forwards, but also as a means of keeping the audience on their toes. Looking back, there was a danger that they relied too much on the gimmick of swapping roles rather than simply telling a good story. In my experience, if a play is to last, it must have a strong narrative as well.

A Man in a Box was a departure from this formula. It was a two-part play about celebrity: the first focused on Colin, an obsessive autograph-hunter, and the second on the crowds who flocked to see David Blaine as he starved himself in a plexi-glass box near London's Tower Bridge in September 2003. Rather than a community, it followed a single man – Colin – and his relationship with his family, and unlike all of my previous plays, the actors in it did not double-up. Instead, each played a single character throughout. Half of the time taken to make the play was spent interviewing a whole host of characters around the subject of celebrity, but in the end I returned to Colin, who was the inspiration for the piece. Far from being a waste of time, the interviews, many of which never made it into the final cut, confirmed for me that his material was very strong indeed. It was exciting to discover that the technique could be used to create such a different play. If the characters and their own personal dilemmas were strong enough, I found that I need no longer rely on changes in location and the introduction of new characters as a way of pushing the narrative forward.

•

In this sense, *The Girlfriend Experience* is the furthest removed of all my plays from the formula established by *Come Out Eli*. Not only does it focus on one small group of women, but it is all set in the same place: the living-room of the brothel where they work. It is where the girls hang out between bookings, watch TV, freshen up and chat. Ideally, I want the audience in the theatre to experience what I experience – an intimate encounter with an otherwise secret world – so I adopt a 'fly on the wall' approach and try to blend into the background. But, of course, it is not possible to spend eight hours in a room with the same people and not participate in some way. The very fact that I am present creates a different dynamic, but even if I was merely 'observing', I'm sure the girls would have got sick of me and put an end to my visits. In order to sustain my relationships with them, it is vital that they enjoy having me there. It is a transaction of sorts: they are giving me their stories, it is only fair that I give them something in return, or at least be relatively fun to be around. While I am conscious of not interfering with the action or altering the mood too much, I am not just a voyeur, I am also a participant.

There have been times when I have had to sit back on my impulse to be involved. One day I arrived at the brothel to find one of the girls on her hands and knees trying to assemble a rowing machine. The other girl working at the time was lounging on the sofa, sipping a glass of sherry. My instinct was to help out, which I did for a while, but then I realised that I was altering the dynamic between the two girls, so I stopped helping and stepped back to observe. On the one hand, this made the situation worse for the poor girl trying to put the rowing machine together all by herself, which I felt bad about. On the other hand, the scene on stage would be a more truthful depiction of the relationship between the two girls.

I would not deliberately interfere with a situation in order to create conflict, but not participating sometimes actually intensifies a confrontation, making the performed scene more dramatic. *Cruising* follows Maureen, a seventy-three year-old widow, who is looking for love online. By the time I met her, she had notched up forty-four dates in two years with no success. When her best friend Margaret got engaged at seventy-six, however, Maureen was sceptical about the match. Knowing Maureen to be the type of woman who speaks her mind, a celebratory toast with Maureen and the happy couple seemed like a potentially rich dramatic meeting to record. I had briefed Maureen beforehand, explaining that I didn't want to lead the interview in any way, and that, as I wanted to be simply a witness to the event, I would try to say as little as possible. I had not had the opportunity to explain this to Margaret, though. In the event, some of Maureen's comments towards Margaret's future husband were quite barbed, and when things became awkward my instinct was to defuse the situation. As Margaret looked at me in amazement during Maureen's attack, I wanted to give her some support, but I had to bite my tongue. It was precisely at those moments when I wanted to interfere with the situation that the drama was at its peak. The reason I felt so uncomfortable was that my presence was actually adding to Margaret's embarrassment. It was great for the heat of the scene but not great for Margaret.

I had never before experienced such divided loyalties. In order to get people to talk freely, it is important that they do not feel judged, so I always try to understand the interviewee's point of view. Someone could tell me they are a murderer, to which my response would be: 'Oh, right, tell me about that then.' Consequently, I often end up forging close relationships with the people in my plays. For both Margaret and Maureen, I had become someone in whom they confided and trusted. But it is only by constantly shifting my loyalties that I am able to tell everybody's side of the story.

Because I am interested in worlds I do not normally inhabit, I have to find a point of connection with each of my subjects that transcends the barriers between us. *The Girlfriend Experience* has led me to a world where I feel the starkest contrast of backgrounds and lifestyles. The simple fact that I am the only person in the room not wearing a negligee and suspenders sets me apart immediately, not to mention my age, background and job. In order to bridge this gap and create bonds with the women, I have to open up more than I normally would. I am rarely aware of this at the time. During interviews, my focus is always on trying to accommodate the subject and make them feel at ease with me. Occasionally, I may steer an interview in a certain direction, but ideally the interviewee leads and, hopefully, all sorts of unexpected things take place that I could never have imagined. In this sense, one has to give up control over the conversation. Perhaps it was inevitable, especially considering how involved I become when gathering interviews, that on one occasion, I unexpectedly found myself becoming a character in my own play.

I had presented a rough cut of *Come Out Eli* at the Actors Centre, and some of the feedback suggested that more pathos was needed. I decided to approach the man who had been held hostage by Eli Hall during the siege, thinking that his story could provide just that. What I got was precisely the opposite. After the initial phone call, in which I explained the project to him, I decided to record our subsequent telephone conversations, because what he was suggesting was so surprising: in return for his interview, he wanted either money, which I did not have, or sex, which I was not willing to give. After three half-hour phone calls, we finally agreed that he would receive lunch, £50 and no sex.

During the interview, the hostage told me that Eli Hall had requested to have sex with one of the female police negotiators, so I realised he was actually copying his captor, and at the end of our four-hour meeting, which provided an extraordinary insight into life inside the besieged flat, he propositioned me again. His advances provided so many clues as to who this man was and what he had been through that I included them in the play. In order to include them, I had to become a character too. To protect myself from any legal repercussions I only included my side of the telephone conversations, because he didn't know that I was recording it. At the time, though, I had made sure that my half of the conversation would make clear to an audience what he had been saying at the other end of the line. The play opened with Alecky on the phone, rebuffing his advances. I think this worked well because it challenged the audience's expectations immediately, and in just the same way that it had challenged mine, but by using myself as a character and presenting the making of the play within the drama itself, I was also letting the audience in behind the scenes and involving them in a way that they weren't used to. This technique of showing the audience how the play was made helped a great deal in gaining their trust.

In one of my subsequent plays, *All the Right People Come Here*, which was a study of class hierarchies, set at the Wimbledon tennis tournament, I became a character in order to give the narrative a stronger arc. Without a ready-made story to follow, the play was instead about my quest to climb from drinking beer with the ticket touts, to having cream tea in the member's enclosure, to meeting Roger Federer himself. Using myself as a character also sharpens the narrative in ways that are often impossible otherwise. As with my telephone conversation, I can use my questions for crucial exposition, containing factual information in them that might not be clear from the interviewees' responses alone.

In its early stages, I toyed with the idea of including myself in the *The Girlfriend Experience* too. Unlike other such establishments, the parlour operates without anyone to answer the phone and open the door to punters. The girls were doing these jobs themselves, to keep costs down. Having heard their spiel when they were on the phone to potential clients, I thought it might be a job I could do. It seemed like a great way of getting even closer to the story, but the logical conclusion of that particular storyline would have been for Alecky, having gone from dramatist to maid, to go from maid to working girl. It was certainly insightful to meet face-to-face the extraordinary range of men who visited the parlour, and it would certainly have been one hell of a story, but it was not a story I was prepared to tell – even for the Royal Court.

Mark Wing-Davey always said that a good interview will cost the interviewer. On one occasion, an interview briefly cost me my sanity and my safety. During the time that I was performing in *Come Out Eli*, I would sometimes go down to Blaine's plexiglass box at night, buzzing from the show. My first taste of success was fuelling my eagerness to find the next big story and turn it into another hit. One night I got into conversation with a down-and-out, who scared and intrigued me. His eyes were a very cold blue – the eyes of a killer, I thought – and when he started to talk about the time he had spent inside, my suspicions seemed confirmed. I was drawn in by his vague references to hunger strikes and top-secret reconnaissance missions. All fired up, my ambition made me all the more daring, and even though his stories scared me, I wanted them to be true. I had never met anyone like this before.

Sensing how personally involved I was with my work, though, he started to provoke me with patronising comments about my career. For the first time, I became emotionally involved in an interview. We left the main compound and went to sit on a bench away from the crowds. It was two o'clock in the morning, so I was a little worried about what might happen, but I was so convinced I would get a great story that I took the risk. What really scared me was the effect that he was having on my mind. By now, he had convinced me that he was part of a powerful organisation, which I assumed to be the IRA as he had a strong Irish accent, and I believed that I was going to be followed. By the time I left two hours later, I had ended up with no real story at all. Instead he had asked me to meet him on the same bench at three o'clock the next day, when he would tell me everything – a story which he promised would make me very rich. It may sound ridiculous that I could have been taken in by him, but I tortured myself over whether to return the next day. In the end, I opted to retain my sanity and stay home, but I was so scared by the encounter that I could not listen to the tape for a couple of months afterwards.

When I did eventually listen to the recording I realised that I had some great material. My journey from confident, chatty woman to scared, vulnerable girl was frightening to listen to. It took me a while to summon up the courage to let anyone else hear it, as I felt so exposed by it, and I desperately wanted to edit out the most embarrassing sections, but of course these were also the most compelling. One of the elements that made it so powerful was that it was happening in the present. Rather than hearing about an event retrospectively, as is so often the case with an interview, the audience could actually witness it for themselves. *A Man in a Box* ended with the man telling me to turn my microphone off, which I did immediately. The audience were left wondering what happened. Did Alecky escape unhurt? If the story were told retrospectively, the audience would know that Alecky was safe in the end. By capturing the meeting in the present, while it was happening, the in-built suspense was maintained.

In this encounter, I had inadvertently overcome two of the biggest challenges of verbatim theatre: how to incorporate dialogue into a verbatim play, rather than relying purely on monologues, and how to escape the confines of retrospective story-telling and include action that takes place in the present. It confirmed something that I had learnt when I first started making verbatim theatre: there is a danger that you only ever get the characters' thoughts and opinions, which lack emotional colour, because the very fact that they are being interviewed makes them conscious of presenting themselves as they wish to be seen. Mark Wing-Davey had often encouraged me to interview people while they were in the midst of some sort of activity, something that distracts them from the microphone and takes their minds off the fact that they are being recorded. The material I recorded for *Come Out Eli* during the siege itself had an incredible energy to it for precisely this reason: everyone's attention was focused on the besieged flat and the hordes of armed police running past. As a result, the interviewees' speech was spontaneous and uninhibited.

At the same time, people were continually talking to each other, not just to me, so I was able to record conversations and moments of live exchange rather than just monologues. Recording actual dialogue rather than interviews can simply be a more immediate and therefore more powerful way of telling the story, but it is also about giving the characters more realism and depth. The audience gets to know a person far better by seeing them interact with their colleagues and friends rather than just with me. When Geoff and Margaret, Maureen's friends in *Cruising*, announced their engagement, I immediately drove to Herefordshire to record their celebratory drinks party. It would be far more powerful for an audience to witness the scene than to hear about it retrospectively. Of course, it's impossible to be 'on the scene' all the time, but the more time you spend with your interviewees, the greater your chances of capturing those extraordinary moments. *The Girlfriend Experience* follows the narrative of the girls' lives and their relationships with one another as they unfold, so it has been developing gradually over the course of a year. When I'm unable to be at the parlour myself, the girls have agreed to record themselves in my absence. This is the ultimate way of creating a non-pressurised, non-interview environment.

•

Even so, *The Girlfriend Experience* is not a documentary and does not pretend to be one. Although my plays are created from recorded life, the characters' words have been processed at so many different stages before they reach performance that by the time they are spoken in a theatre they have taken on a life of their own. The first stage – the edit – is where the creative process really begins. Again, this is aided by the use of audio rather than visual recording, which allows for far greater flexibility when manipulating the material into a narrative structure. Unlike a visual documentary maker, whose material will, by its nature, be strictly bound to the time and place where it was recorded, I am able to link fragments of material to form a continuous narrative. I'm always mindful of taking something so far out of context that it distorts the way in which the comment was originally intended, but it is not an easy task to cut fifty hours of material down to an hour, while maintaining one's integrity, and still to tell a good story with it. While cutting and splicing material does give it more impact, there is the danger that a character is whittled down in order to fit the story, rather than generating the story themselves. I am always faced with the same struggle between remaining faithful to the interview and creating a dramatic narrative.

The people who agree to be recorded for my shows are entrusting me with their stories, which are often very personal, so I do feel a great responsibility to present them in a way that they are happy with. At the same time I have a responsibility to the audience to present them with a good evening's theatre. A successful play will strike a balance between the two. Although they do not have final approval over what is used and what is cut, I try to explain to my interviewees that the recordings will be edited, that they are being used to create a piece of drama, not their biography, and I try to keep them informed of any significant changes that I am making to the material. No matter how much I have prepared them, though, I am always nervous about their reaction when they come to see a show, and I can tell when I have pushed the edit too far, as I tend to break out in a cold sweat.

This was certainly true of *I Only Came Here for Six Months*, a commission for the British Council in Brussels that explored the social tensions between fat-cat earners at the EU and the indigenous Belgian population. It was a kaleidoscope of stories that lacked a strong narrative, so clashes of opinion were the main source of conflict and drama. One of my fat-cat interviewees spoke so eloquently about his right to a high salary that this material made it into the final draft even though the rest of his interview didn't. Unfortunately, from his point of view, I ended up editing out many of his more endearing qualities, one of which was that he had married a Belgian and was actually incredibly well-integrated within the Belgian community, setting him clearly apart from the stereotype. I regret that I presented only one side of him – his less attractive side – but if I had presented him in a more balanced light, the impact of his speech would have been diminished. Despite feeling a little stung when he watched the play performed, he actually enjoyed it immensely, and even goes so far as to call himself a fan.

The competing demands of truth and drama were most fiercely opposed when I adapted *A Man in a Box*, my play about Colin the autograph-hunter, for television. In the theatre, one tends to have a more sympathetic, or at least a more captive, audience. The television producers were concerned that the edited interviews simply weren't dramatic enough to keep people tuned in, so they encouraged me to write fictional scenes to include within the verbatim drama. Having never actually written dialogue before, I found this a very scary prospect. We met to brainstorm ideas. The script editor did a marvellous job of refereeing the meetings, while the director suggested possible story-lines and scenarios, which I rejected with my 'truthometer'. Eventually, I lowered the level of truth on the gauge and started buying into the heightened dramatic narrative that the producers and director required.

I had buckled, and with some regret. The first part of the programme, which was ninety per cent verbatim, worked better than the second, which included more fictional material, and the two parts felt out of kilter with one another. When his father died, Colin realised the importance of his family, which he had been neglecting, and found a stronger bond with his own son. The director wanted to show Colin reaching crisis point and losing control of his senses, so I wrote a scene that showed him lashing out at his best friends. The film was shot in the style of a 'mockumentary', with the characters talking to a documentary maker (me) standing behind the camera. It was possible to imagine Colin reaching a state where he might do such a thing, but I would never have actually witnessed that kind of behaviour. The very basis of the programme – the device of the relationship between the interviewer and the interviewee – had been distorted. No wonder the scene was unbelievable and sat uncomfortably within the rest of the programme. I wish I had trusted my instincts more.

Another near-disaster was the director's decision to allow the actors to add 'ums' and 'ers' wherever they felt it was appropriate. The audio had been painstakingly transcribed with every 'um', 'er', stutter and non-sequitur lovingly preserved, because it is these that reveal the person's thought processes: there is always a specific reason why a person stutters on a certain word, and it is this detail that gives the characters such startling verisimilitude. Not only was this lost, but it slowed the actors down impossibly. Fortunately, this note was retracted before we started filming.

Working in television made me realise how much freedom and creative input is afforded to the writer in the theatre. That said, the show will only blossom in the hands of a good director, and inevitably a good director will bring a whole host of ideas to the table that will shift the piece yet further from the recorded actuality.

Having tried my hand at directing a couple of shows, I have realised how much a play can improve with the help of a fresh pair of eyes. My first play, *Come Out Eli*, was the one that came closest to recreating the real-life scene as it actually happened. As time has passed, I have become less literal and far less purist in my approach to verbatim. I find myself moving further away from the reality of 'how things actually happened' in my quest to create a dramatic narrative. For example, in *Cruising* there is a scene in which two couples are chatting in a pub. In reality, the interviews with each couple took place in different pubs at different times, but in an attempt to unite their two plot-lines, Matthew Dunster, the director, suggested we place them in the same pub. It worked brilliantly. It is harder for me to make imaginative leaps like this because I am so married to the truth of what actually took place and I am very cautious when it comes to changing contexts like this, so it is really important to find a director who shares my sense of integrity, but I think it is perfectly valid to take a liberty such as this one, which is not going to upset any interviewees.

At the same time, my productions have also become more naturalistic, in that they tend to adhere more closely to the unities of time and place. This is mainly to do with making plays that focus on a smaller group of people in fewer locations, allowing me to use costumes, scenery and props much more. Part of the joy of watching the earlier, multi-location plays was that when a character first started speaking, the audience would have no idea where they were until, for example, he shouted 'Bill, please!' across the stage, and it suddenly became clear that he was in a restaurant. The minimalism of their staging – few props, little costume, abstract set design – drew the audience's attention by withholding this sort of information. This is not possible with *The Girlfriend Experience*, which is a chamber piece: every object that is used in the recorded material must appear as a prop. This isn't an aesthetic choice, it's simply the best way of telling the story.

Another effect of working with fewer characters is that I have moved towards casting to type. In the earlier, ensemble pieces, the most memorable characters tended to be the ones who were played by an actor of a different colour or gender from the interviewee: the contrast between what they were saying and how they appeared subverted stereotypes and challenged the audience's preconceptions. People's words become all the more resonant when they are coming from the mouth of a person you would never expect to be saying them. For example, in *Come Out Eli* Don Gilet's most eye-catching performance was as David

Field. Don is black, mid thirties and exudes contemporary cool. David Field, on the other hand, was a genteel retired solicitor from the Home Counties, who spoke in a measured upper-class voice, occasionally breaking into perfect Latin. In fact, the actors would usually be cast against type. When each actor is only playing one character, though, cross-gender and cross-race casting is less attractive because it can interfere with the naturalism of the production.

Developments in technology have helped to disguise the practicalities of the recorded delivery technique – the actors' use of headphones, for example – from the audience, or at least make it less intrusive. For *Come Out Eli*, each actor was equipped with their own minidisc player, and at the top of the show all of them had to press 'play' at exactly the same time so that they were in synch. When it came to duologues, though, a split-second's difference between recordings could throw the timing of the whole scene, so it was important for both of the actors to be plugged into the same machine. Sometimes this meant having long extension cables sprawled across the stage. Most recently, when we did a scratch performance of *The Girlfriend Experience*, the actors used in-ear monitors that were linked to the sound desk via a radio signal, so no wires or plugging in and out of machines was necessary. This makes for a much slicker performance, and gives the actors more freedom to move around without having to 'plug into' the person they are having a conversation with.

On the other hand, the audience quickly forgets that the actors are working from an audio feed, which I think is important. The play should be strong enough to stand up on its own, but it becomes all the more poignant when the audience knows that it's created from real life recordings. (More importantly, if the audience did *not* know that the words were real I would feel like I was conning them. The audience has a right to know where the material comes from.) To counteract this, at the beginning of the performance, the audience is able to hear the recorded material over the theatre's PA at the same time as the actors are listening to it through their earphones. For the first few seconds, the recorded voices overlap with the actors', before gradually fading out and leaving only the voices of the actors, who continue to hear it through their earphones. Even though the recorded delivery technique is a very simple idea, it is not that simple to explain through performance. Exposing the mechanics of the recorded delivery technique in this way seemed to be a relatively effective means of showing the audience what was going on.

The acting techniques required by my work suit some actors more than others, particularly those who have a comic touch – although this may simply be because I'm drawn to interviewing colourful characters. For them, it is just a matter of getting the brain into gear, and after that it's down to the same skills needed for conventional acting. However naturalistic the staging, though, what the audience sees is not the actual location, and however accurately they've been cast, the actor is not the actual interviewee. Now they must present what was recorded privately and in the intimacy of an interview to an entire audience. Even though they attempt to copy every detail of pronunciation and rhythm of speech, the text goes through another, final stage in the process that gives it a life of its own.

•

I am more interested in drama than journalism, and the dramatic thrust of a play will often displace precise factual representation. I now find myself moving even further from the strict verbatim approach that I began with five years ago. Each attempt at crafting a narrative from recorded material has led me to bolder editing and staging, and further from the 'truth' of how it actually took place. *Come Out Eli* was a gift of a story that I was lucky enough to capture. The material was so rich with narrative that it did not require the same degree of manipulation that I have found necessary with some of my subsequent projects. In fact, in most cases, the hours of research and recording that go into making a verbatim play do not lead to a satisfying story, and in retrospect I am not surprised that, because of this limitation, I wrote fictional scenes for *A Man in a Box*. Although this is not something I would necessarily have done had I not been working for television, I found the creative freedom of these fictional scenes liberating, and I am inclined to develop this skill.

I do not mean to say that I am no longer dedicated to the verbatim technique. At the least, it is a wonderful tool for generating extraordinary performances of riveting real-life characters, and in some cases it can provide insight where journalism fails. Actually hearing someone's words being spoken in the manner in which they were said offers a much fuller picture than reading a transcript of those same words in a newspaper. But like any form of theatre, verbatim needs to keep reinventing itself in order to keep thriving. Even though it serves political drama particularly well, it should not be limited merely to this genre. I want to surprise audiences by using the verbatim technique in new ways and by experimenting with its use in different genres. An audience wants to be entertained, and this means being gripped by a story which facts and journalism – and 'pure' verbatim – may not be able to provide.

So I feel pulled in opposite directions. On the one hand I yearn for more control over the drama, which makes the incorporation of fictional scenes very attractive. On the other hand, how could I ever hope to write anything that comes close to the fantastically rich and multi-layered messiness of real speech? How could I ever write anything as good as real life? I had an enormous battle with myself when writing the fictional scenes in *A Man in a Box* for this very reason. For me the challenge is to try to marry the gorgeously unwieldy nature of real speech to the dramatic needs of the story without losing the very thing that makes verbatim so magical, its life of its own.

RICHARD NORTON-TAYLOR

Richard Norton-Taylor is Security Affairs Editor for the *Guardian* newspaper. His 'tribunal plays', which dramatise public inquiries for the stage, include *Half the Picture* (1994), *Nuremberg* (1996), *The Colour of Justice* (1999), *Justifying War* (2003) and *Bloody Sunday* (2005). *Called to Account: the Indictment of Anthony Charles Lynton Blair for the crime of aggression against Iraq: a Hearing* (2007) used a similar form to dramatise a fictional inquiry using verbatim testimony from real witnesses. All were first performed at the Tricycle Theatre. He has also written many books investigating the abuse of power in public agencies.

The Tricycle Theatre's acclaimed pioneering of verbatim theatre, or tribunal plays as we prefer to call them, began on a tennis court in North London. It was an accident, simply chance. I treated this first encounter with theatre as an experiment; the serious motivation – the realisation that we were onto something with the potential to inform and empower audiences – came much later. In fact this working relationship, begun while Nicolas Kent and I played tennis together, proved to be the catalyst for a series of plays which raised consciousness about contemporary scandals and, in the view of many critics, revived political theatre in Britain. For me, the experience has shown just how powerful and how complementary to journalism – in many ways how much more effective than journalism – the theatre can be.

It was 1994. Nicolas Kent, the Tricycle's artistic director, had been reading my reports in the *Guardian* on the long-running Scott 'Arms to Iraq' inquiry, convened to establish whether the government had followed agreed procedure in relation to defence exports to Iraq. Richard Scott, a senior judge (and now a law lord), and his counsel Presiley Baxendale were relentlessly interrogating present and former ministers, including Margaret Thatcher, senior diplomats and civil servants. Not, one might think, promising material for a stage show. The story had no physical action, no surprises, very little movement, and not much of a plot.

But it had something else. It had dissembling, buck-passing, hiding behind euphemisms, word play, facetious use of aphorisms and, above all, the cynicism and amorality of arrogant and unaccountable officials. Like all our tribunal projects, the play dramatised the methodical process of cutting through these layers of duplicity; it examined different versions of events until an accurate, though not always orderly, account emerged – *Guardian* theatre critic Michael Billington called this the 'raw information'.*

Despite initial misgivings – my own as much as anyone else's – our staging of the Scott Inquiry was heralded as a major success. I was genuinely surprised by the good notices it received. The critics seemed to treat the play as a refreshing change from conventional theatre. And during our staging we exposed the truth about the 'Arms to Iraq' scandal – or at least, the closest any public report had got to the truth; certainly closer than I could have got as a journalist. Exposing the truth has been the goal of each of our tribunal plays, and my aim here is to examine how we have gone about achieving that goal, and why the tribunal form has been a successful means of doing so.

•

We called this first play *Half the Picture*, a phrase taken from the cross-examination of David Gore-Booth, former British Ambassador to Saudi Arabia. Baxendale asked him about answers drawn up by officials and ministers to parliamentary questions from MPs. This is an early exchange in the play:

---

* *State of the Nation* (London: Faber and Faber, 2007), pp 384–5

BAXENDALE

If there is a question, it should be fully answered, should it not?
The answer should be sufficiently full to give a true meaning?

GORE-BOOTH

Questions should be answered so as to give the maximum degree
of satisfaction possible to the questioner.

BAXENDALE

I am not sure you really mean that, because it is rather like
people just giving you the answer you want to hear, I think is
what you have just said. I do not think you quite mean that.

GORE-BOOTH

No, it might be the answer you do not want to hear.

BAXENDALE

That does not give you much satisfaction. Should the answer be
accurate?

GORE-BOOTH

Of course.

BAXENDALE

And they should not be half the picture?

GORE-BOOTH

They might be half the picture. You said, should they be accurate
and I said, yes they should.

SCOTT

(*Intervening*) On a more broad approach towards answering
questions, there would be nothing the matter with an approach
which proceeded on the footing that you would in every case be
as forthcoming as you could?

GORE-BOOTH

Correct. But there are often cases in which you cannot be so
forthcoming, for reasons of what are called foreign policy.

Later Sir Robin (now Lord) Butler, the cabinet secretary, told
the inquiry that 'half the picture could be true'. Scott warmed
to the theme with a former foreign office official, Mark Higson,
who resigned because of the Thatcher government's refusal to
come clean with Parliament: 'There is a distinction between a
half truth and an untruth. Your seventy-five per cent is not a half,
it is a three-quarter truth. Then there is an untruth, which is just
not true. It is not a question of just being true to a point.' But
Ian McDonald, a Ministry of Defence official who had been the
government's spokesman during the Falklands war, told Scott:
'Truth is a very difficult concept.'

Truth may be a difficult concept, but the search for it and the
denial of it have been constant themes of our tribunal plays. In
1996, two years after *Half the Picture*, I edited *Nuremberg* to
mark the fiftieth anniversary of the world's first war crimes trial.
This was just as the UN tribunal into war crimes and genocide
in the former Yugoslavia was beginning in The Hague, and we
performed *Nuremberg* alongside short, specially commissioned
plays on more recent crimes and massacres – including the war in

the former Yugoslavia,* and the genocide in Rwanda – to remind us that man's inhumanity did not end, even in Europe, with the defeat of the Nazis.

Each defendant at Nuremberg had repeated the oath: 'I will speak the pure truth and will withhold and add nothing.' One of *Nuremberg*'s main themes, both at the original trial and in our play, was the extent of and justification for 'complicity in the lie', as the journalist and broadcaster Sheena McDonald put it.[†]

Denial features strongly in *The Colour of Justice*, first staged in 1999. The police officers questioned in the Macpherson Inquiry repeatedly insisted they were not racist – that their attitudes were in no way influenced by the fact that Stephen Lawrence was black.[‡] The play's impact was enormous. It gave a real boost to the resurgence of verbatim theatre. People may have heard or read snippets about the circumstances surrounding the murder of Stephen Lawrence but they were unaware of what it revealed and its implications. Watching the recreation of the inquiry opened people's eyes to what Billington called the 'negligence and reflex racism of the British police'.[§] The play highlighted a potent issue and provoked anger; it brought a wave of youngsters, many of them black, into the theatre for the first time; it was put on the syllabus of police colleges, and is regularly performed in schools.

---

*   Nicolas Kent later produced *Srebrenica* based on The Hague tribunal's evidence of the massacre of Muslims there

†   'Nuremberg retrials', *New Statesman and Society*, 24 May 1996

‡   At the time of writing (spring 2008), no one has been convicted of Stephen's murder

§   'Hindsight Sages', *The Guardian*, 29 December 1999

The play struck a particular chord in Northern Ireland. The common theme was the attitude of the police: in England, explicit or implicit racism; in Northern Ireland, prejudice or even hostility towards Catholics. When *The Colour of Justice* played in Belfast, many commentators compared the murder of Stephen Lawrence to that of Robert Hamill, a young Catholic beaten up as officers of the Royal Ulster Constabulary, it was alleged, simply looked on. Of the many murals in Belfast, one, on the Omagh Road, is of Stephen and Robert, side by side.

During the Saville Inquiry into the events of 'Bloody Sunday', which I adapted for the stage in 2005, soldier after soldier, advised by the Ministry of Defence, repeated the mantra 'I can't remember'. The circumstances were very different but there were echoes of the responses given by the white youths accused of killing Stephen Lawrence. Again, notions of truth and accuracy became the subject of careful debate. Barry MacDonald, a lawyer representing the families, asked Soldier S (all the paratroopers were allowed to remain anonymous, and some gave evidence from behind screens) about a witness statement in which the soldier said nail and acid bombs were thrown at the paratroopers from the top of the flats in Derry's Bogside:

MACDONALD
That was false, was it not? You did not see any nail bombs or acid bombs being thrown?

SOLDIER S
I would not say it was false. It is inaccurate.

After the soldier said he saw 'objects' being thrown, MacDonald asked, 'Did you see any nail bombs or acid bombs?'

SOLDIER S
No, I did not.

MACDONALD
Why did you suggest these things?

SOLDIER S
Because of the nature of the way the things were done at the time.

Under hard questioning from Michael Mansfield, also a lawyer for a number of the victims' families, one paratrooper broke down and admitted shooting Barney McGuigan, one of the unarmed civil rights marchers.

In 2003 a bitter row blew up between Alastair Campbell, Blair's chief spin doctor, and the BBC over Andrew Gilligan's claims that the government's weapons dossier on Iraq had been 'sexed up'. The government was determined to expose David Kelly, its weapons scientist and expert on Iraq, as Gilligan's source, leading to great anguish on Kelly's part at appearing to have misled the Commons Foreign Affairs Committee by not telling all he knew about the affair. Following his suicide, the Hutton Inquiry was set up 'urgently to conduct an investigation into the circumstances surrounding the death of Dr Kelly', and *Justifying War* was a distillation of the verbatim evidence it collected. Whether it resolved the matter of whether the government was responsible for his death or not, the discredited weapons dossier at the heart of the inquiry clearly demonstrated that, compared to denial and contradiction, exaggeration and omission were far subtler but equally potent means of distorting the truth.

Until 2006 we had based our plays on material from official inquiries. In 2007, for *Called to Account*, we went a step further and set up our own inquiry, examining the case for the indictment of Tony Blair for the crime of aggression against Iraq.*

We were surprised at the number of people who agreed to be questioned, by the lawyers Philippe Sands QC and Alison Macdonald for the prosecution, and Julian Knowles and Blinne Ni Ghralaigh for the defence. They included a former top official in the Ministry of Defence, a former appeal court judge who had also been a commissioner responsible for monitoring the intelligence services, former ministers and UN ambassadors, and Richard Perle, notorious neo-con and former adviser to Donald Rumsfeld, the US Defense Secretary at the time.

The infamous weapons dossier provided the background of this investigation, too, but we structured the play around the evidence of Michael Smith, a journalist who had been leaked a series of highly classified Downing Street and cabinet office documents showing how Blair and his advisers, and the Bush administration, had duped the public and plotted to manipulate the case for war.

The documents demonstrated that Blair was hiding important truths from Parliament, notably concerning what he told

---

* There may yet be an official inquiry, when all British troops have left Iraq, into the way the Blair government took the country to war in 2003

President George Bush about his commitment to join the invasion of Iraq – just as, years before, as *Half the Picture* showed, the Thatcher administration had withheld important information from Parliament. It was fitting, perhaps, that we returned to Iraq, the subject we started with for our first tribunal play. As we reminded those who accused us of ignoring the crimes of Saddam Hussein by putting on *Called to Account*, we were among those who exposed the British government's hidden deals with him in the first place.

There was no hard evidence that Blair could be charged with war crimes. But in *Called to Account*, as in the other tribunal plays, we presented the facts, leaving, as the playwrights of ancient Greece did, the audience, in the role of the jury, to make up its own mind.

•

There are many effective weapons available to those determined to prevent the truth from emerging. They include dissembling, euphemism, deliberate ambiguity and plays on words. Civil servants, diplomats and government ministers are past masters at it. Watching them work with these tools can be both compelling and infuriating, but in most situations, including answering questions from MPs and journalists, they succeed easily in their aim of concealing the truth. It is different when individuals are forced into the limelight and questioned by judges, or even by lawyers, in an inquisitorial context as opposed to an adversarial trial. Notice the distinction between a trial, in which one party is seeking to triumph over the other by attaining the desired verdict, and an inquiry, in which the aim is to uncover and establish the most accurate version of events. If our intention has always been to expose the truth, then we have been helped in this because the format we have recreated, namely an inquistorial tribunal of inquiry, has precisely shared this aim. Moreover, I believe that our tribunal plays have been able to expose not only the truth of a given situation, but also the attitude of mind, the intellectual sub-culture, of individuals in positions of power and authority. The stage is perhaps better suited to portraying these casual evasion tactics than any other art form or medium of communication.

Such tactics can be entertaining, and even provide comedy. In one scene in *Half the Picture* Tristan Garel-Jones, a foreign office minister, contradicts himself by explaining that in the government's view the disclosure of any sources or alleged sources of intelligence information would cause 'unquantifiable damage' to the country's security and intelligence agencies.

The damage could be 'both unquantifiably great and also minuscule?' asks Scott.

'Yes,' replies Garel-Jones.

In the same play Andrew Leithead, a government lawyer, eloquently reveals Whitehall's secretiveness: 'It is damaging to the public interest to have the decision-making process exposed.'

'Any decision-making process?' asks Baxendale.

'Any decision-making process,' replies Leithead.

This is not just word-play, fun and games for the middle classes. The exchanges reflected the true mindset at the heart of government, revelatory in a way a press or television interview would never be. Others have indulged in this mendacity: in *Nuremberg*, Alfred Rosenberg, the Nazi philosopher, argues over the meaning of *Ausrottung* (extermination). 'I do not need a foreign dictionary in order to explain what various meanings in the German language the word "Ausrottung" may have,' he tells Thomas Dodd, the American Assistant Prosecutor, who has asked him to look up and read out to the tribunal the definition of the word. Rosenberg continues: 'One can exterminate an idea, an economic system, a social order and, as a final consequence, also a group of human beings certainly.' Reminded that he used the word in the context of the Jews, Rosenberg replies: 'We are speaking here of extermination of Jewry; there is still a difference between Jewry and individual Jews.'

Disingenuous disputes over meanings and definitions also feature in *The Colour of Justice*. In a telling exchange Stephen Kamlish, representing the Lawrence family, asks Linda Holden, a detective constable responsible for liaising with the Lawrence family after the murder, 'What was your view as to the motive for Stephen being killed at the time you were acting as a family liaison officer?'

HOLDEN
I was obviously aware that it was a racist murder, but what the motive was I couldn't say.

KAMLISH
Is not racism a motive? A motive is racism?

HOLDEN

Yes, that's right.

KAMLISH

Stephen was killed by a bunch of sadistic racists. Do you not accept that?

HOLDEN

I do, but I can't say what was in their minds at the time.

KAMLISH

Do you accept he was killed because he was black?

HOLDEN

I really can't answer that.

Michael Mansfield QC, the Lawrence family's lawyer, presses John Davidson, a detective sergeant involved in the investigation into the teenager's murder, on this crucial point:

MANSFIELD

I do not want to debate with you about the nature of racism, but do you recognise that thugs who may kill white people for a variety of reasons, but who kill blacks because they are blacks are committing a racial crime?

DAVIDSON

Yes, sir, I recognise that if they were killed because they were black, that is racist.

MANSFIELD

That is exactly what this case was about but you refused to recognise it, did you not?

With what he might have thought was an unanswerable response, Davidson replied: 'I still refuse to recognise it, sir. I am very surprised that anybody knows it is about that because it has never been cleared up anyway, sir.'

•

In striking contrast to the practised defiance of certain witnesses, official inquiries – and, through them, our plays – have sometimes been granted access to information or attitudes never originally destined for the public. Frightened of being accused of a cover-up, the government passed to both the Scott Inquiry (*Half the Picture*) and the Hutton Inquiry (*Justifying War*) sensitive internal documents. Such discoveries make the process of putting on these plays even more compelling and illuminating.

Half the Picture used revelatory material to show that the attitudes of the British and American governments towards Saddam Hussein in the 1980s were very different from the one they adopted when they invaded the country twenty years later. The breathtakingly cynical – some would say the realistic and properly self-interested – approach was expressed by William Waldegrave, a foreign office minister, in a document used by Scott to question witnesses at his inquiry, and included by us in *Half the Picture*:

'I doubt if there is any future market of such a scale anywhere,' Waldegrave told his government colleagues in a briefing about the situation in Iraq in October 1989, 'where the UK is potentially so well placed if we play our diplomatic hand correctly, nor can I think of any major market where the importance of diplomacy is so great on our commercial position. We must not allow it to go to the French, Germans, Japanese, Koreans et cetera. The priority of Iraq in our policy should be very high in commercial terms, comparable to South Africa in my view... A few more Bazofts or another bout of internal repression would make this more difficult.'

Government policy was to increase the supply of arms and arms-related products to feed Saddam's voracious appetite. His gassing of the Kurds at Halabja in 1988 and his arrest, and later execution, of Farzad Bazoft, the *Observer* journalist, were events the government put to one side while pursuing this lucrative trade. This was a secretive business, and in fact the export of arms to Iraq only came to light because of the collapse of the prosecution, by zealous customs officials, of directors of Matrix Churchill, for breaching export guidelines. Matrix Churchill was a machine tool company privately encouraged by government ministers to trade with Iraq, whose director, Paul Henderson, was working as a spy for MI6. The furore following the trial's collapse led to the Scott Inquiry. Held largely in public, the Inquiry continued intermittently for the best part of two years. It was reported even more intermittently, an experience I found as a journalist very frustrating.

Often, the internal documents reveal the extraordinary efforts to which officials and ministers go, not in deciding the substance of policy, but in determining how to present it. A document handed to the Hutton Inquiry, and used in *Justifying War*, quotes a senior official warning Downing Street about the controversial – and now known to be inaccurate – dossier the government drew up on Iraq's weapons programme as part of the build-up to the invasion of Iraq in 2003: 'The existing wording is not wrong,' he says, 'but it has a lot of spin on it.' At one point, Jonathan Powell, Blair's chief of staff, told Alastair Campbell, 'We need to do more to back up the assertions.' The two men later discussed – by e-mail – the exaggerated claim that Saddam could attack Britain with weapons of mass destruction within forty-five minutes of giving an order to do so. Powell wrote: 'Alastair, what will be the headline in the *Standard* on the day of publication [of the dossier]?'

'Search me,' Campbell told the Hutton Inquiry when asked about it. He was reminded that the London *Evening Standard*'s front page headline was '45 Minutes From Attack'.

'Did you have any hand in the headline?' Campbell was asked.

'I did not. I do not write headlines for the *Evening Standard*,' Campbell replied. This, too, was less than the full picture: Campbell might not have actually written newspaper headlines, but he was certainly able to influence them.

A notorious example of how Campbell influenced the media occurred in February 2003, a month before the invasion of Iraq. He handed political correspondents a dossier on Iraqi weapons claimed to be based on secret intelligence information but in fact taken mostly from an academic thesis publicly available on the internet.*

At one point, James Dingemans QC, counsel to the Inquiry, asked Campbell about an e-mail that had been sent to him.

DINGEMANS
You have Tom Kelly here, the Prime Minister's official spokesman, writing an e-mail saying: 'This is now a game of chicken with the Beeb – the only way they will shift is [if] they see the screw tightening.' Was this the mindset that was dominating Number 10 at this stage?

CAMPBELL
I do not think it does reflect the mindset really. I think I know what Tom is saying there. I think e-mails that are sent between colleagues who are very close and work together very closely can look very different when you are staring at them in a screen in a courtroom.

It was not until after the invasion of Iraq in March 2003 that the true picture began gradually to emerge. Officials leaked to newspapers minutes of Downing Street meetings and telegrams about meetings between US and British officials, discussing how

---

* See, for example, 'How Saddam hides illegal weapon sites: Blair to reveal spy dossier of videos and phone taps. Saddam Hussein is using an elaborate network of deception to frustrate the United Nations' weapons inspectors and conceal Iraqi weapons of mass destruction, according to new intelligence documents released by Downing Street.' *Observer*, 2 February 2003. Other examples of Downing Street's manipulation of the media when Campbell was the Prime Minister's Chief Press Secretary can be found in *The Rise of Political Lying* by Peter Oborne (London: Free Press, 2005).

to prepare for the invasion. These revealed that in March 2002, a year before the invasion, Christopher Meyer, Britain's ambassador in Washington, told David Manning, Blair's foreign policy adviser, that he had told the White House, 'We backed regime change. But the plan had to be clever and failure was not an option.' He went on to talk about 'the need to wrong-foot Saddam on the [weapons] inspectors'.

Minutes of a Downing Street meeting from July 2002, chaired by Blair, revealed that 'C' (for Chief, as the head of MI6 is officially called within Whitehall – at the time Sir Richard Dearlove) reported on his recent talks in Washington: Dearlove warned that 'military action [was] now seen as inevitable, Bush wanted to remove Saddam through military action justified by the conjunction of terrorism and WMD, but the intelligence and facts were being fixed around the policy'.

We, the public, did not know what was being hatched behind the scenes at the time; nor did Parliament, nor did most members of the government. The leaked material quoted above was the subject of a front page story in a single newspaper on a single day – long after events had moved on. Documents released in this way often lack context, and can seem isolated or no longer relevant, but our staging of *Called to Account* brought them together and made sure they were shared by a wider audience.

•

I wasn't long into my new career as a tribunal playwright when I realised just what scope the theatre had, compared to what we now call the media: newspapers, radio and television. What before might have been written about haphazardly in short newspaper articles, or mentioned all too briefly in television and radio news bulletins, could be put together into a coherent piece of two hours or more – incorporating thousands of words. A theatre audience could listen together and inwardly – indeed outwardly – digest and understand properly what all the fuss was about. The perforce brutal and inconsistent editing, the constant fight for space or air time, is one of the many problems of journalism as a medium.

The theatre can be an extension of journalism in the best possible way – that is, by communicating and explaining contemporary issues, scandals and events in a unique, fair, positive and intellectually honest manner. Formally, tribunal plays make use of one particular advantage. There is an inbuilt conflict to the proceedings, with both sides giving their version of events, usually determined to stick to their position, but sometimes breaking down and confessing.

Actor William Hoyland, who has appeared in all of our tribunal plays, gave an evocative description of this process in 2004. He was referring to the Tricycle's verbatim drama *Guantanamo: Honor Bound to Defend Freedom** (the title was taken from the inscription above the entrance to the US camp in Cuba). We have heard and read about Guantanamo in dribs and drabs, he said. 'Here it is condensed in one evening, alive in front of your eyes. It has a much greater impact both intellectually and emotionally.' Nicolas Kent observed: 'You [the audience] are communing

---

* by Victoria Brittain and Gillian Slovo. See page 150.

silently with your fellow human beings with a multitude of different voices alive for you.'

We demonstrated, said Sheena McDonald, commenting on *Nuremberg*, 'that theatre can reach those parts of the mind apparently cauterised by media coverage [...] by focusing on the word. The investment of time and concentration needed to watch and hear is repaid with a terribly enhanced understanding of the human capacity to hurt and deny responsibility.'[*] David Hare identified the 'enhanced understanding' provided in *The Colour of Justice*, saying it 'laid before a live audience all the subtleties and intricacies of British racism, all its forms and gradations, with a clarity which I had never seen emulated by television, documentary, or newspaper'. He described the play as 'a rebuke to the British theatre for its drift towards less and less important subject matter' and praised 'the sheer seriousness and intensity with which it was able to bring the theatre's special scrutiny to bear'.[†]

All this praise is very pleasant for the writer, of course, but I include it here rather because it shows something important about the specific qualities of tribunal theatre. Three things emerge from these comments. First, that there is a specific power in watching something played out in front of you. A group of actors on a stage can draw back the curtains of Whitehall, or those of any other powerful authority, and give a sense of context much more effectively than can the written word alone.

[*]   MacDonald, op cit

[†]   See 'Why Fabulate?' in *Obedience, Struggle and Revolt* (London: Faber and Faber, 2005)

The experience of watching leads to an understanding that goes beyond the mere intake of information; it involves empathy for the victims. Second, that witnessing the search for truth and the exposure of injustice as a group of spectators places a corporate responsibility on the audience to acknowledge that injustice – and, potentially, to act to prevent similar future injustices. Third, that there is a genuine hunger to engage with political material in a serious, unsensationalised manner – and that the stage is the perfect place to do so.

Many of the above qualities of tribunal theatre became evident during the staging of *Nuremberg*. Amid the charges and counter charges, Sir Hartley Shawcross, the chief British prosecutor,[*] read out the harrowing testimony of a witness to a massacre of five thousand Jews.

'I well remember a girl,' said the witness, 'slim and with black hair who, as she passed close to me, pointed to herself and said, "Twenty-three." I walked around the mound and found myself confronted by a tremendous grave. People were closely wedged together and lying on top of each other so that only their heads were visible. Nearly all had blood running over their shoulders from their heads. Some of the people shot were still moving. Some were lifting their arms and turning their heads to show that they were still alive. The pit was already two-thirds full. I estimated that it already contained about a thousand people. I looked for the man who did the shooting. He was an SS man, who sat at the edge of the narrow end of the pit, his feet dangling

[*]   Sir Hartley Shawcross, H M Attorney General 1945–51

into the pit. He had a tommy gun on his knees and was smoking a cigarette.'

Shawcross was reading, but reading aloud on the stage – using material with much more effect than if the same words had been read in a newspaper or even a book. A live audience concentrated and listened – and became horrified – together.

•

The first problem of composing verbatim theatre from long public inquiries or tribunals is deciding what to include. The editor has the formidable task – an almost physical struggle – of distilling tens of thousands of words spoken over many months, and in some cases years, down to the relatively few that can be filtered through the mouths of actors in little more than two hours. A journalist would instinctively choose the key revelations or disclosures, accusations and arguments, and also use examples to illustrate the main themes. Revelations make exciting viewing, but I learned through Nicolas Kent that a theatre audience also wants changes in tone and tempo. He encouraged me to include scenes that would not normally interest a journalist because they seemed so inconsequential and didn't move the story on. In fact they offered telling insights.

Edmund Lawson QC, counsel to the Macpherson Inquiry, asked Inspector Groves, a senior police officer who arrived at the scene soon after the stabbing of Stephen Lawrence, if it was correct that he had no surviving notes.

GROVES

No, sir, I have not.

LAWSON

There was reference to you having a clipboard at the scene?

GROVES

I still have the clipboard. I don't have any notes.

Michael Mansfield QC, counsel for the Lawrence family, later asked Groves when he took his notes back to the police station.

GROVES

I am not sure.

MANSFIELD

I would like you to think.

GROVES

Well, I have thought about it for five years.

We learned from the inquiry that Conor Taaffe and his wife were returning from church when they saw Stephen on the ground with his distraught friend, Duwayne Brooks. Taaffe was honest enough to admit to the subconscious stereotyping that is widespread in Britain and elsewhere. He was asked whether he thought they might be about to commit a mugging.

Taaffe replied: 'The thought flashed through my mind, being wary of the situation, that perhaps it was a ploy. One would fall down and you would think: "Oh, my God, there's something wrong."

You would go over and the other might get you. That did pass through my mind.'

He described how his wife cradled Stephen's head and spoke in his ear. 'I thought it was such a lovely thing for her to say because Louise and I both knew that hearing is one of the last things to go, and so, while he was there, she said: "You are loved. You are loved." I had some blood on my hands. When I went home – this isn't material but I will say it anyway – I went home and washed the blood off my hands with some water in a container, and there is a rose bush in our back garden, a very, very old, huge rose bush – rose tree is I suppose more appropriate – and I poured the water with his blood in it into the bottom of that rose tree. So in a way I suppose he is kind of living on a bit.'

Stephen's mother, Doreen, described how when she went to the police station she handed an officer a piece of paper with names of suspects written on it. She continued: 'He took the paper from me, he folded it in small pieces in his hand, and then he had it in his hands like this, crunched it up in his hand like a ball, and he held it like that, and as I was walking out through the door, I said to him: "You are going to put that in the bin now, aren't you?" And he was shocked because he didn't realise I was watching him, and he quickly said: "No, we treat all information that comes to the police."'

One of the potential dangers while editing *The Colour of Justice* was diminishing the seriousness of the issues the Macpherson Inquiry raised by indulging in caricature, a kind of music hall treatment of the police officers on stage as, consciously and unconsciously, they exposed their racism, prejudices and incompetence. Including the apparently mundane details of some testimonies added light and shade to what might otherwise have become a crude depiction of inhuman officialdom. In the event, one senior and sympathetic Scotland Yard officer who attended the first night said I had been 'too fair'.

•

I have already indicated that my confidence in the theatre was not there at the beginning. Watching the early rehearsals of *Half the Picture* at the Tricycle, I thought we were heading for a humiliating disaster. How 'untheatrical' it all seemed. I need not have worried. Nicolas's judgement and foresight were to prove right – indeed inspired. I was converted to the theatre, and to actors. The cast, which soon took to the collective name of The Tribunal Players, were asked to do what they had never done before – that is, not to act in the conventional sense, but to recreate as faithfully as possible the original – the body language, the inflections, the expressions of the people they were portraying on stage. Nicolas has always been careful to avoid caricature and impersonation. Verisimilitude was and is the key. One government official was overheard asking his mother after watching and listening to himself portrayed by an actor in *Half the Picture*, 'Wasn't I good?'

Nicolas encouraged the cast to attend the inquiries to see the process for themselves. When they couldn't, many of them met the individuals whom they were to play on stage. The actors realised they were also doing far more than simply entertaining: they were messengers performing, without being at all preachy, what we all believed was an extremely valuable role before an appreciative audience, who were sharing an experience that appealed to the intellect as well as the emotions, as they heard what human beings have done to each other in the past, and what they still can do to one another now.

•

Some still question whether such pieces of verbatim theatre can be called plays at all. The issue has become the subject of a running debate, especially in the wake of the success of *The Colour of Justice*. Criticisms have included: questions over whether a recreation of a tribunal qualifies as a play at all; complaints that the plays have a specific agenda and are therefore a simplification of the issues; the fact that they are not created in the same sense that an imagined play would be (for example, that the writer did not invent the lines the characters speak).

The debate over the status of our tribunal plays as 'proper stage material' seemed to be resolved when the shows won a string of awards, including an Olivier Award for 'outstanding achievement'.* The productions were finally acknowledged to be true theatre and not an abuse of the stage.

The question of simplification is more difficult. I have explained here that a two hour stage presentation lies in a convenient space somewhere between the several months (or even longer) of tribunal testimony and the cursory reports offered in the daily media. Our plays are not comprehensive but they are representative. I have also explained the lengths to which

* Presented by the Society of London Theatre

Nicolas Kent and I have gone in order to include in our plays the complexities of the inquiries.

But is making a tribunal play a creative act? True, I do not think up a story, nor do I write dialogue. The choices I must make are different from those of a writer who begins with a blank sheet of paper. Editing – as in writing verbatim drama – may seem more of a craft than an art. I quote David Hare again:

'It is true,' he said, 'that the dialogue in *The Colour of Justice* was, as it were, "found". Norton-Taylor [...] did not actually have to waste time in the tedious business of giving characters lines, any more than the sculptor sits rusting iron or degrading driftwood. But in his faultless act of organisation and selection, he has done precisely what any artist does. By Picasso's great criterion, Norton-Taylor did not paint a tribunal of a racist crime. He painted the anger you feel when you look at a tribunal.'*

To be honest, *pace* Hare, I do not regard myself as an artist. However, I find it interesting how differently a play is perceived from a newspaper article. I am frequently asked when I am going to write another play or what the next inquiry to be staged might be; such questions are rarely asked about the next article or exposé. This may reflect the status given to those who write for the theatre, not to mention journalism's low esteem in the public's mind.

I have discussed our tribunal plays here as tools for the exposure of injustice and subterfuge, as an extension of journalism in

*   Hare, op cit

another form, and as a means of providing insight into hidden processes and scenarios. The Tricycle's tribunal plays set out to provide information, to explain and expose, and to provoke debate. But they address broader issues – honesty, truth and the accountability of those who have power over us.

For some younger members of the audience, *Nuremberg* may have been the theatre as educator. For others it brought back memories. One member of the audience, whose family members had died or were gassed in Auschwitz and concentration camps elsewhere, broke out in tears as she berated me at the end of one evening's performance for upsetting her so much. Why then did she come, I asked myself? These are serious issues, but they are also emotional subjects.

There is much talk of verbatim theatre being 'honest', 'accurate' or 'truthful', but I hope that we have also shown that the theatre can be subversive – as much so as any journalism. I hope that our plays continue to be regarded as important, at least in showing how the theatre can confront contemporary issues in a unique way. With the exception of *Nuremberg*, our plays have indeed dealt with current controversies – scandals – and have shed light on the society in which we live. They might still be held up, performed even, in the future as a yardstick to judge whether lessons have been learned, or just as a reminder of what people have had to put up with.

NICOLAS KENT

Nicolas Kent is Artistic Director of the Tricycle Theatre in Kilburn, North London. He has commissioned and directed many 'tribunal' plays, which dramatise official inquiries for the stage. These include *Half the Picture* (1994), *Nuremberg* (1996), *Srebrenica* (1997), *The Colour of Justice* (1999), *Justifying War* (2003) and *Bloody Sunday* (2005). In 2004 he co-directed the verbatim play *Guantanamo: Honor Bound to Defend Freedom* and in 2007 he staged *Called to Account: The Indictment of Anthony Charles Lynton Blair for the crime of aggression against Iraq – a Hearing*, a fictional inquiry using verbatim testimony from real witnesses.

[The following interview was conducted by Will Hammond and Dan Steward on 16/09/07.]

STEWARD

In your introduction to the published script of *Srebrenica* you
write, 'I was so upset that this testimony to the worst massacre
in Europe since World War Two was receiving so little public and
media attention that the editing of this material into a play for
the theatre became a necessity.'* Would you say that this sense of
obligation has been behind all of your verbatim theatre work?

KENT

Yes, it often stemmed from my feeling that there was a large
injustice somewhere that needed highlighting, or a piece of
history that was somehow obscured and needed some light shone
on it – particularly with Srebrenica. When we did the Nuremberg
play, Richard Goldstone[†] came to the Tricycle performance
and said to me, 'You must go over to The Hague and watch the
Rule 61 Hearings against Mladic and Karadzic because seats will
be like gold dust; there's going to be a huge reporting on this
because Mladic and Karadzic are going to be called to account.'
I went to The Hague – he having facilitated my seat to get
in – and I found five or six people in the courtroom. And I was
so dismayed by this, as I listened to the evidence – which was
extraordinary. I just couldn't believe that this was not a huge
story. Here we were, an hour and a half's flight from London, and

---

[*]   Nicolas Kent, *Srebrenica* (London: Oberon Books, 2005), 5

[†]   Chief Prosecutor for the War Crimes Tribunal for ex-Yugoslavia

no one was reporting on this hearing *in absentia* for Mladic and Karadzic. The first person who'd been found guilty of being part of that massacre, a soldier, had given evidence about taking part in a mass execution. It was on the news every night in Holland because Dutch troops had been there – it was the leading story. I came home and thought all the newspapers would be full of this. I listened to *The World Tonight*, and there was the tiniest item at the end of the news just saying that the hearing had happened. And the next day I got all the newspapers, and there was nothing in any newspaper except literally about fifty words in *The Financial Times* tucked away somewhere. And that was all the reporting there was.

It seemed to me appalling: here was something about the United Nations having failed to act to protect a safe haven; about the international community having allowed this massacre to happen and not even trying to bring to justice the two people who'd perpetrated it, Mladic and Karadzic. There had been the hearing in The Hague and international arrest warrants had now been issued, but there was no attempt to get justice within the media, or to get a groundswell of opinion. As we now know those two arrest warrants still have not been served; ten years later these two people are still at large. The international community was not galvanised by this, and I thought, 'This must get to a wider public.' So it became a necessity to do something about it and to do it through verbatim. It seemed the only way to do it, because here were four days of transcripts which could quite easily be put into a play. It didn't actually take that long to edit – I think I spent maybe two weeks putting that play together; it showed me how easy it was not to walk by on the other side.

STEWARD

So when you felt the compulsion to write – or to put together – *Srebrenica*, as well as the other plays you've done here at the Tricycle, what would you say you hoped to achieve?

KENT

I think I hoped to illuminate the particular issues that the enquiries or trials were addressing. With *Srebrenica*, it was very important to look at the way the European Community, the United Nations, the peacekeeping force, the British public, all of us had not really understood that what was going on there was a genocide. It had become convenient to stand back and say, 'Well, this is a safe haven.' We were going to protect these people but we didn't actually do that; we said, at the beginning, that this is a safe haven and we will look after these people – and then the international community just walked away. Here was the biggest massacre in Europe since the Second World War. Eight thousand had died, and somehow no one had actually looked at what happened, no one had looked at the way the United Nations hadn't functioned, at all, effectively. No one had said, 'This must not happen.'

STEWARD

You have often presented material from public inquiries in an edited form as an evening's drama. Does the theatrical presentation of them get this material out in an accessible form?

KENT

The problem with public inquiries is they're very ill-attended, they're rarely broadcast on television, or any other broadcast medium, so as a result, very few people see them. When you go into a public inquiry you find there are five or six people in there on a boring day and on a sensational day – if Margaret Thatcher is attending the Scott Inquiry, for instance – there might be a hundred people. But that's it, and out of a population of fifty-five million that's obviously an extremely small percentage. Then you get a very cursory, edited version of what happened in the newspaper which normally runs to five or six hundred words. You have to wait to read the report at the end, the conclusions of the judge or the inquiry panel, which again is a summary of the evidence and the conclusions taken from it. But you don't hear the evidence in detail. Now obviously if you're only putting two hours on the stage of a nine-month inquiry it's a very selective edition, but it's quite often a much longer edition than the public have received through the press and the media because instead of the sound bites or the quick reports of about one or two hundred words, they're getting someone's whole line of argument, if you address it well.

STEWARD

Are there other advantages in presenting it as a play rather than, say, a piece of written journalism?

KENT

You get a very good overview with a play because obviously you're looking at the inquiry after it has finished, rather than in the day-to-day way that the media report. You can see what the most important evidence is, and prioritise that evidence, whereas if you're looking at it day to day, one day seems important and then the next day might contradict it and seem equally important, but you can't weigh one against the other until after the event.

And there is a sort of storytelling. Any inquiry is rather like a good courtroom drama, because they always follow the same narrative form: you lay out the circumstances first, then what happened, and then the reaction of the authorities to what happened, and then the examination of whether those people reacted correctly or incorrectly; then they come to some form of conclusion within the inquiry before the inquiry report is written. So, having started at the very beginning with a very open view of what happened, they're trying at the very end to be conclusive. This lends itself to a drama very effectively, because you have a beginning, a middle and an end.

The other thing that lends itself to the theatre is the cross-examination process, because it is often a process of conflict and it's obviously very interesting for people to see someone state something with enormous confidence, and then to see a lawyer disrupt that confidence, or make them reconsider the evidence, or get to the truth. I think what particularly rivets an audience is trying to sort out the truth. By watching how people give evidence, the way they react to questioning, I think an audience feels that they are empowered and able to arrive quite dispassionately at the truth in their own minds.

HAMMOND
Richard Norton-Taylor has worked with you on several tribunal plays. Can you explain how your working relationship with Richard came about and how it operates?

KENT
Well, I suppose *Half the Picture* was the first one. I used to play tennis with Richard and he would regale us with stories of the

Scott 'Arms to Iraq' Inquiry – he'd been there almost every day – and it was always interesting, but in the end you thought, 'What are the issues?' I'd read quite a lot of the daily reports about the Scott Inquiry, but there wasn't an arc that gave you an understanding of the whole situation. We played tennis one summer's day, and afterwards I went home and I opened the *Observer* and the *Sunday Times*, and the main editorial in both newspapers said words to the effect that, when the Scott Report was published at the end of the inquiry, it would probably be the most important constitutional document of the latter half of the 20th century. And I thought, 'I'm getting anecdotes about Margaret Thatcher and Alan Clark and I don't quite see it: what's so important about this? If two major newspapers are saying this then presumably there is some truth in it somewhere.'

So I rang Richard and I said, 'What about doing this whole thing on the stage?' He said he was writing a book about it, but I wanted to do it on stage. I grabbed various other people and talked to David Aukin [film producer and co-founder of Joint Stock], and he thought it was probably a good idea, and then I got John McGrath to write some fictional pieces to go between the inquiry scenes and finally persuaded Richard to edit the whole thing. When they heard we were doing the Scott Inquiry, one bright spark in the box office here at the Tricycle said, 'Well, that'll be a good time to take a holiday, because two men and a dog are going to book for this show.' But it just took off in a most extraordinary way.

Richard then had the idea of doing a verbatim re-enactment of the Nuremberg trials. It was the fiftieth anniversary of the hearings and that seemed to be a very good time for a reassessment. Another reason was that in 1996 there was no international war crimes court, and it was unthinkable that there would be one. We used Richard Goldstone's address marking the fiftieth anniversary of the Nazi war crimes trial as a curtain-raiser, in which he explained how necessary it was to have an international criminal court. I remember a very powerful two-page article by Sheena McDonald in the *New Statesman*,* saying how important watching *Nuremberg* as a play was, because it made her realise how far away we still were from having a world order with an international criminal court, and that surely this was the time to create one. Well, four years later the Rome Treaty came about, and suddenly an international criminal court was set up, and several years later Charles Taylor from Liberia was being tried. So there was a huge sea change in people's thinking and in legal processes. I know America still hasn't signed up to it but most countries have; America will sign up eventually, undoubtedly. I'm certain we were a very, very minute part of that whole sea change of thinking.

I thought *Nuremberg* would be very difficult – it was something Richard wanted to do. Agreeing on which witnesses to use to tell the story was quite complicated, because there were so many. I was very keen to put Shawcross's closing speech in the play,† which was very important, and Richard's first version didn't have it. That's been the good thing about working together: his first version was rather anti-dramatic, and the Shawcross speech is very, very dramatic, it's an absolutely wonderful speech, it's one of the great speeches of the 20th century. I suppose there

---

* *New Statesman and Society*, Vol 9 Issue 404 (24 May 1996), pp 22–3
† See page 109

is a slight tension between us, with me looking for slightly more dramatic material and Richard always hoeing the path of truth and non-bias. But that tension is useful.

The Stephen Lawrence play, *The Colour of Justice*, came after great pressure from me to get him to do it. I remember I was at the airport, about to fly to France on holiday and I read in the newspaper about the Nation of Islam creating a demonstration at the Macpherson Inquiry into the death of Stephen Lawrence when the suspects gave evidence; I read a very graphic account – written by a playwright actually, Dolly Dhingra – who'd written from her own personal point of view because she'd been there that day. I was very moved, and I phoned Richard Norton-Taylor from the airport and said, 'We have to do something; we can't not do the Stephen Lawrence Inquiry, we're missing a huge story here, an important story.' And I rang Richard every day from France. He didn't want to do it because he was too busy, but finally he gave in. I think he even cancelled a holiday to do it, but he did it, perhaps just to get some peace and quiet from me!

Bloody Sunday Richard was absolutely desperate to do. Hutton [*Justifying War*] I had to push him very hard. And *Called to Account* we both were of a mind to do. I think it was my idea, but he suggested Philippe Sands and it was very much a joint project.

STEWARD
Are there any subjects or inquiries which you have wanted, but been unable, to tackle?

KENT

I think we've done everything that we wanted to do. I've been offered hundreds of projects; everyone rings me up about something different. I've always said I'm not prepared to do inquiries that don't really impinge in some way on the way we live now and have a wider application – a wider interest – for society. For instance, I didn't do the David Irving prosecution because it had more to do with Irving than the Holocaust, and we'd in fact dealt with that to some extent with *Nuremberg*.

STEWARD

In previous plays the tribunal had already happened, the material was extant. But with *Called to Account* you had to generate the material yourselves.

KENT

It was very different. It was really the three of us: myself, Richard and Philippe Sands, who was very important. Philippe has an extremely good address book; he has a lot of very close, very good contacts and he put quite a lot of pressure on people. I wrote the initial letters and Philippe followed up. Then there were one or two breakthroughs: I got Clare Short, and Philippe very much helped us get Richard Perle and Michael Quinlan, who was very important to us because even though he's not very well known in wider circles, he was the Permanent Secretary to the Ministry of Defence. The minute people in the establishment knew he was taking part in this process suddenly everyone was willing to take part because it was like a seal of approval. So we then got people like Edward Mortimer, who was Kofi Annan's communications director, and all sorts of people like that.

STEWARD

When you were putting together your list of interviewees were you aware of the issue of balance in who you were asking?

KENT

Yes, very aware. And it was very difficult to find people who would defend Tony Blair's position. I mean really difficult. The people we did get to defend his position then eroded that position, like Richard Perle, who came up with a statement at the end about the intelligence being wrong but adequate, or Michael Mates, who really didn't put up a very good defence for Blair, I thought. We had a lot of people who backed out at the last minute, like Ann Clwyd, who suddenly said she didn't want to be part of it; and Lord Owen, who was very pro the war, looked like he was going to do it and then suddenly said no. It had become a very unfashionable position. And I think they saw the Prime Minister on the way out so there was no particular advantage in defending him.

STEWARD

It's interesting you mention that – did you feel that once you'd decided to do it you needed to do it as quickly as possible?

KENT

We had to do it before Blair left Parliament. I was never going to do it after he'd left Parliament. It was interesting that the minute he announced the date of his resignation the box office went down, just slipped away. I think a lot of the audience for that show saw it as a sort of catharsis; people felt they'd gone on the demonstration and their voice hadn't been heard and they wanted to be part of something that actually put a government on trial for taking us to war on an inadequate basis. It was almost like getting even. I mean, a majority the audience was certainly biased; I don't think the show was, but I think there were very few Blair supporters in the audience.

STEWARD
Do you sense that you're preaching to the converted at times?

KENT
That doesn't worry me. Because if you preach to the converted what you're often doing is strengthening the converted. I think maybe eighty per cent of the audience are already decided on some subjects, such as Blair. I would say less on things like Stephen Lawrence or Guantanamo, where people are seeking more information. On Blair I suppose eighty per cent know their position before they come into the theatre, but when they leave their position is possibly more entrenched and strengthened. So let's say that eighty per cent have become more vociferous and are engaged more with the democratic process – if you strengthen people's resolve to do something about an injustice or a lack of democracy, it means that the next time we're confronted with the possibility of taking action against, say, Iran, you're going to have a few more people saying, 'Hey, wait a minute, what does the intelligence actually show? And is this legally defensible?' Now, that's not a bad state of affairs.

Now, of the other twenty per cent, let's say five per cent think they're coming to see a musical called *Called to Account*; well, they're going to learn something, which is great, or they're going to get bored stiff and walk out. And fifteen per cent might be coming because they are interested and haven't made up their mind but are just curious because people are saying, 'Well, you should go and see this thing.' That's also terrifically worthwhile because fifteen per cent is thirty to forty people per night whose opinions might change and who might learn something. Well, that's wonderful – I mean, you can go to political meetings and there are five people there.

STEWARD

Do you think there were people who came to *Called to Account* who were against the war and thought that Blair had misled people, but who came away from it doubting the evidence against him?

KENT

There were, I think, a lot of people who thought he would have gone down in a court of law who then, having seen the play, saw it was a more complex situation. And there's nothing wrong with complexity in the theatre, with coming out and still wrestling with the issues. I think that's rather good, if you come out and think, 'Well, actually, on what basis could you charge him?' This will affect the way you frame laws in the future. It was interesting that Philippe Sands went through a journey doing this play: I think he was quite certain that Blair could be prosecuted for a crime of aggression against Iraq, and I think he came away slightly less certain of that. For example, there was a long argument about *mens rea*, which is a huge legal argument about whether or not you had intended to mislead – what was in your mind. It's deeply complex but it's about whether Blair deliberately set out to mislead, knowing that he would commit an illegal act in doing so.

HAMMOND

There's a moment in *Called to Account* where Philippe Sands presses whoever he's talking to for a distinction between deceit and dishonesty, which is quite a subtle distinction; is that what that related to?

KENT

Exactly. There was a day when thirty-nine e-mails flew back and forth between the defence and prosecution lawyers, and people were not on speaking terms for some days at the end. It resolved itself but it became unbelievably dramatic off-stage as we were formulating the 'count' to be used in the play. There was a sort of argument about what the 'count' was.

HAMMOND

Were the opening and closing speeches written?

KENT

They were written, but we edited them because they were very, very long; they were about ten minutes and fifteen minutes and we had to cut them back severely.

HAMMOND

In Michael Billington's review of *Called to Account*, he wrote, 'At least the theatre has now called Blair to account.'* Would you say that that's enough? In other words, how do you measure the success of any of your productions? Do you ever feel you've achieved what you hoped to? Obviously something like *The Colour of Justice* became a big national event.

* *Guardian*, 24 April 2007

You can only measure the success of these plays by whether you illuminate the arguments and make people understand things they didn't already understand; whether people are clearer when they leave the auditorium than when they went in. I think with *The Colour of Justice* that did really work. People who had no understanding of the words 'institutional racism' came out at the end and really understood what institutional racism was; they'd listened to the police giving evidence and suddenly realised that the police came from a position where they thought that black people were inferior to white people and they were not giving them the same justice. Duwayne Brooks, for instance, who was one of the victims: they were treating him as if he was a suspect from the very beginning of that inquiry right through to the end; their position did not change. So when people saw that play they really began to understand what it was to be black and to be a victim – you were dealt with differently. There's a moment in the play when one of the senior police officers talks about 'the attitude towards coloured people' – despite it already having been established that black people found the term 'coloured' offensive. When we performed the play at Stratford East, suddenly everyone in the audience started to jeer this police inspector, because they saw that he was still anchored back in the race relations of the 1950s or 60s. When Macpherson came out and said 'This is institutional racism' (and that was when the phrase, effectively, entered the British psyche), when the reports said that, I think there was a sea change in the way Britain was policed.

I think the play fostered a great feeling of solidarity from an audience against institutional racism. I talked to people who said, having seen the play, their attitude had changed. If they saw a black person being stopped by the police they would ask why these people were being questioned, just to be a witness to what was going on. People came out feeling that this was something they'd understood and something they would make sure wouldn't happen in the future. There were also a lot of black people who came to see the play and sat in an auditorium alongside white people, and they suddenly thought, 'You are beginning to understand what we have been through.' And I think by watching the actors playing Neville and Doreen Lawrence on stage, reacting to evidence, but not actually giving evidence, you began to understand what that family was going through. Through empathy, I think, people learned an enormous amount watching that play.

Similarly, with *Bloody Sunday*, the audience actually put themselves in the situation of the victims; those who had been shot and injured, who, as the inquiry revealed, were demonstrating peaceably, and then were attacked as terrorists by the army, fired at without any justification at all.

HAMMOND

You said in an interview with Terry Stoller that the Tricycle Theatre has a sizeable local black population and a sizeable local Irish population. So those two plays were a great fit for the Tricycle and had a corresponding success. Have there been tribunal plays where you've felt frustrated at the lack of response, and if so why might that have been?

KENT

The Colour of Justice and *Bloody Sunday* had the strongest
reactions, because they were about personal issues; both inquiries
were set up to right wrongs for people who'd suffered grave
injustices. The Scott Inquiry, and to some extent the Hutton
Inquiry, were slightly drier – there was a grave injustice because
Kelly was dead, but the inquiry was about more than his death.
Despite their dryness I don't think these two worked less well,
because the audience came out angry, or felt that the government
had behaved in a cavalier fashion, in both cases. In the arms
exporting case, everyone felt that this was a government who'd
acted deceitfully, exporting arms and encouraging the export of
arms and pretending that they were not. In the same way, in the
Hutton Inquiry, everyone thought that the dossiers had to some
extent been sexed up, although I think the evidence is somewhat
circumstantial, but certainly Kelly was pointing to the fact that
more emphasis had been put on things than the intelligence could
actually bear.

STEWARD

One slightly different example would be *Guantanamo*, not a
tribunal play in the same way, but a verbatim play. Obviously the
issue was ongoing when *Guantanamo* was staged here because
the British terror suspects were still in Guantanamo Bay. Did the
play have a campaigning element to it?

KENT

Guantanamo was blatantly a campaigning piece of work, yes,
against the injustice of holding people indefinitely in detention
without trial and without any charge. And we were looking
particularly at the British people who'd been held there, British

residents and British nationals, although we were also looking globally at what happened and the justification for Guantanamo in the American administration's mind. But, yes, it was a campaigning play and it's one that did raise awareness, I think, tremendously. We actually played it at the Houses of Parliament and we even played it on Capitol Hill. And I think it did make a very, very slight amount of difference. It raised awareness, and I think it did contribute in its way to the release of the remaining British nationals, of whom there were five when the play was on, and the British residents, a couple of whom have been released recently, one of whom was represented in the play; we were very actively campaigning for his release.

STEWARD

Some people have said that because verbatim theatre has a specific agenda, it takes a simplified approach to complex issues. Is that a legitimate criticism? Is it a relevant criticism? And are you aware of this when you're programming the plays and producing them?

KENT

Verbatim theatre's always going to be simplified because it is only a number of views – it can never be the whole picture. It's political theatre and it's engaging with contemporary society, and dealing with incredibly complex issues. If you're going to put complex issues into two hours or an hour and a half you're going to have to simplify them, that is certainly true so I accept that criticism.

I've never been a great exponent of verbatim theatre, ironically – I say that with a slight grin because the form is not something

I feel that strongly about. For me verbatim theatre has been a means to an end, it's been a very good way to tackle issues I've wanted to tackle. Together with Richard, or with Gillian Slovo and Victoria Brittain, people who care about injustice, we've managed to fashion plays using verbatim. It's been a way of making plays to deal with certain issues, but it's literally been the means to get there, it's not that I believe it's a finer form of theatre. You can respond more quickly with verbatim than you can with a fictional drama; this is more like a living newspaper and it's a faster process.

The other benefit of verbatim is that you get two sides of the argument very quickly portrayed, both of which are totally believable because they're what those people said, whereas, if you did it fictionally, you might blunt the argument, or obfuscate or exaggerate the argument. On a political issue or an issue of justice it does help to hear what people actually said.

STEWARD
So how do you feel about plays which combine verbatim text with invented dialogue or invented scenarios?

KENT
I thought you'd come onto that. I absolutely don't like that form at all. I find that form slightly dishonest. I would rather have total fiction. If you mix the two you lead an audience to believe that someone said something they didn't actually say. The strength of verbatim theatre is that it's absolutely truthful, it's exactly what someone said. It may be edited, but Richard and I have always had certain rules when we work together. For example, if someone asks a question, you must never skip to another answer,

you always have to give the answer to that question; you can edit the question a little bit, you can edit the answer a bit, but you've got to keep the chronology going. If you suddenly chuck in something you make up because it's easier, I think you distort the truth – what you come to may be very illuminating but it isn't, in my view, the absolute truth of what happened and what people said. And my attempt, in using verbatim, is always to get as near to the truth as you can.

HAMMOND

On the one hand you have a text which fulfils journalistic criteria for accuracy and truth, but on the other hand you have a play which can be described in dramatic terms, involving protagonists and conflict and classic dramatic structures, which you describe as very useful. Is there ever a conflict between presenting something in a dramatic form, that's to say something which engages the audience, and adhering to that accuracy?

KENT

There's always a conflict, yes, because if you're going to do a public inquiry, or a trial, most of it is incredibly boring. You take out the salient points and the most dramatic points and use those. If you did an absolutely accurate view of the trial, the audience would be bored stiff and they'd be there for nine months. So you can't do that. But you can give an overview that is very coherent. Now, you have to make sure that overview is not biased. It's very important that whatever side you're on – and Richard and I are often on one side of the argument with something we firmly believe – whatever side you're on, you give the other side as good an ammunition as you possibly can, so that it is as unbiased as possible. But you also try to condense it so that the dramatic story is totally clear to people. In a way it's like a précis of the trial, but it looks very carefully at the turning points. As a result you get a very rounded, unbiased overview of the evidence. If you read that evidence in great detail you might get lost, or bored, or you might not quite see its point. In this sense, our version is more coherent, and that's an enormous positive.

HAMMOND
So the need to engage your audience – I hesitate to use the word entertain, but to keep them concentrating and interested – is dealt with by the fact that the script is a condensation, so they're getting the most important moments...

KENT
The highlights.

HAMMOND
And, given how important they are, that in itself keeps the audience focused?

KENT
There will inevitably be some fairly boring detail you have to go through, things you have to lay out so people understand. A good example is Christopher Clarke who, at the Bloody Sunday inquiry, made an opening statement which lasted six weeks; we condensed that opening statement into thirty lines. The statement took you through what he was setting out to show as Counsel for the Inquiry: what had happened on Bloody Sunday, the aftermath, how it was covered up or wasn't covered up. Basically what he was seeking to prove. He took us through the history of the Troubles, effectively: the British army coming in to

Northern Ireland and the beginning of the policing of Derry, and all of that – he was very technical and detailed. But by simply showing the questioning later in the inquiry, one person asking a question and someone answering, by demonstrating the line he was pursuing, it was much clearer than listening to a six-week lecture. With a very short series of questions lasting maybe five minutes, we elucidated two days of peroration.

STEWARD

Given that there's this tension between accuracy and drama, is the process of directing a tribunal play essentially different from that of directing a fictional play?

KENT

The intention of a tribunal play is always, always to try to arrive at the truth without exaggeration, and I think that that informs the rest of my work. I'm always asking, 'Why? Why does the character do this? Why say that? Why?' That's a director's job. With a tribunal play, whenever you do anything for dramatic effect it's wrong, you know it's wrong.

HAMMOND

Do you find yourself restraining your actors from doing what comes naturally – dramatising and projecting?

KENT

For actors it's not like being in an ordinary play. They know they're taking part in something that is to some extent 'history', so they come with such a commitment to the truth and the project that the minute anyone sees anyone else acting, everyone knows – so no one acts; it's like there's an unwritten pledge that in no way will anyone do anything for effect. So the atmosphere is very restrained. We all work very much together, so I find myself being a chairperson.

I've always worked with microphones and with the house lights up, which is an attempt to diffuse the theatricality of the process, so that the audience are in the room with the characters and we're all in it together; the audience's laughter, their anger or their being moved is all part of the same event. And the microphones mean that the actors don't even have to put on a louder voice in order to be heard. The hyper-naturalism of everything being very low-key means it's nearer to the truth, I suppose. It's like the honesty of a film close-up, where if an actor starts to act on a film close-up you can absolutely see it. If an actor is miked and starts acting, it stands out like a sore thumb.

STEWARD
There are even those moments in the scripts when someone says, 'I'm sorry, we can't hear you, can you come closer to the microphone?'

KENT
Yes, and those we deliberately retain. There are lots of little things: 'Can I use a marker pen?' or mentioning the numbers of the documents, where the most mundane stuff makes the whole thing so much more believable and truthful, because you're dealing with actual documents and having to find those documents. There was a moment in *Bloody Sunday* when one of the actors went onto the inquiry website and was following the documents on the website while performing on stage. What we're doing with these public inquiries is very near to the news,

so you're conscious that your character might be in the news tomorrow. That gives it an edge, and it means you must never betray your character.

The actors can be quite possessive of their character, and there are quite some tussles. I had big tussles with Diane Fletcher, who played Clare Short in *Called to Account*, because we had to cut the play down, and she felt that if I cut some of the evidence Clare gave, it diminished Clare's intelligence and understanding of the Middle East and the post-invasion situation in Iraq. She was determined that Clare should have her say, but I also had to make the play shorter. All morning, we were battling back and forth... Now that's wonderful, because people are actually so engaged with their characters that they feel it's necessary to defend their characters' positions. Obviously the editor's position, or the director's position, is paramount because someone has to decide how long the play lasts, but that input is very good, and we've always had that input from the actors. People will come up with something else in the transcript and say, 'Actually, shouldn't that line be in? Because we lose that part of the argument without it.'

STEWARD
Diane Fletcher was widely praised for her imitation of Clare Short.

KENT
But it was quite a way from Clare Short, funnily enough. It was an essence of Clare Short but it wasn't a mimic of Clare Short. She was widely praised for having exactly the same voice,

but when you put Clare and her together the accents are not the same.

HAMMOND

Is imitation one of the things you look for, or do you avoid that?

KENT

I encourage the actors to read all the evidence of their particular character, to get an overview of what their character is seeking to say, and I get them to read as much background about the character as they can – if possible even to meet the character – and then to go for an essence of that character. You often find that as the actor researches, they somehow start to take on the body language of the character. When Thomas Wheatley was playing William Waldegrave in the Scott Inquiry, he read all the evidence and watched Waldegrave a bit because he was a minister at the time and often on television. There was a moment when Wheatley gave evidence as Waldegrave – he started sort of washing his hands while he was giving evidence. And later on when someone saw the play they said, 'How did you know?' This person had been there, he'd watched Waldegrave give evidence, and as he gave his evidence, saying, 'Oh, it's nothing to do with me', Waldegrave had been making gestures as if he was washing his hands. And Thomas, by reading that evidence, by watching Waldegrave, not knowing about the washing of his hands, but just watching the character and getting inside his mind as an actor, he'd created the body language Waldegrave used. Often actors create that body language through a sort of osmosis. It's extraordinary. I don't quite know how it happens.

STEWARD

In these instances where there's someone as well known as, say, Clare Short being portrayed, or Waldegrave at the time, is there a danger that people are judging the imitation and that this can distract from the importance of what's being said?

KENT

That's one of the reasons we excluded Tony Blair from the Hutton Inquiry play. We didn't intend to exclude him from the beginning but we knew it was going to be difficult, and when we examined what he said he actually didn't say anything new, he just stonewalled. To put him on stage would have seemed rather pointless, and it would have led to people saying things like, 'Is that as good an imitation as Rory Bremner playing Tony Blair?' When we did the 'Arms to Iraq' inquiry we had Sylvia Syms playing Margaret Thatcher, and it was a very good…imitation is the wrong word, it wasn't an imitation it was an *essence* of Thatcher; she was fixated about 'guidelines' and 'sticking to guidelines' all the way through. Margaret Thatcher repeated herself and bludgeoned the inquiry, she was very disdainful and really did not want to be questioned in public by a judge, and she made it quite clear she was there on sufferance. Sylvia had got that. But it did, however much one didn't want it to, become a bit of a turn because it was Margaret Thatcher, not because of anything Sylvia did. She was still Prime Minister at the time, or she'd just left office, and people wanted to have a go at her really; so it does become a distraction when you're dealing with someone very famous like that.

HAMMOND

Talking about audiences wanting to have a go at Mrs Thatcher, and also of using what you might call alienation effects in order to keep the audience as grounded in reality as possible, do you think that over the time you've been putting on these plays, audiences' reactions to this sort of play have changed? Was there ever a point when people were entering the theatre not realising quite what they were letting themselves in for?

KENT

They have changed very slightly, I think because of reality television and things like that. But even the style of acting has changed in the last fifteen years. We did the first one in 1994 and acting styles have become even more naturalistic since then. So, for instance, people say 'er' and 'um' an awful lot, but in the first inquiries they didn't; it was much cleaner; we said the lines naturalistically but we said the lines. Now we include 'ers' and 'ums' and stutters. We also have available more of the recordings. With the earlier ones you could never get hold of the audio recordings. I don't think we managed it with *Bloody Sunday* but we obviously managed when we did *Called to Account*, because that was our own inquiry, and we did manage to get some of the audio recording from the Hutton Inquiry. And as we've imitated the recordings to some extent, I think the style has changed.

The audience have been exposed to more theatre like this, so they know what they're going to get. There have been plays such as *The Permanent Way*, or *Stuff Happens*,* or there's been Robin

* Both by David Hare. See page 46.

Soans' *Talking to Terrorists*, or even *Forgotten Voices*.* So people accept that style of doing things.

STEWARD

Do you get a different audience for a verbatim play than for something like *Small Miracle*,† a more conventional entertainment?

KENT

Possibly we do. We get some crossover. For instance an awful lot of lawyers come to the tribunal plays, and we get quite a lot of opinion formers. It's very interesting, the audience. We get the ex-Prime Minister of Peru, or the Foreign Minister of Chile, or the Governor of the Bank of England. All sorts of people come and see these verbatim plays, so they do attract the movers and shakers. I don't want to lose our broad audience base but I like the fact that we attract opinion formers because after all they're the people in power, so if you can change one or two of their opinions, that's very useful. Certainly in the case of *Guantanamo* it's useful, and in the case of institutional racism it's useful; it's even useful when it comes to *Srebrenica*.

HAMMOND

Do you ever invite people to performances who you think either need their mind changing or are in a position to take action?

* Adapted by Malcom McKay from the book by Max Arthur
† Staged shortly after *Called to Account* at the Tricycle

KENT

We hold discussions after the performances. For instance, David Aaronovitch came to the first night of *Called to Account*, as did Menzies Campbell and Jon Snow; so there was a panel afterwards. David Aaronovitch was given a very tough time by the audience. When we do panels we try to have both sides of the argument represented.

STEWARD

So when as a theatre you're marketing a season of three or four plays, is there a conscious decision to market a tribunal play differently from an imagined play?

KENT

Only in that we would also go for an audience interested in current affairs, or even film – people who've seen *Fahrenheit 9/11* or films like that. When we started these verbatim plays there were hardly any documentaries in the cinema, and the explosion in documentary film has been enormous. You have Al Gore's film [*An Inconvenient Truth*], you have *Who Killed the Electric Car?*, you have *Super Size Me*, to name but a very few. There's a dearth of that stuff on television now. You used to have *World in Action*, and plays like *Cathy Come Home*; you used to see four or five documentaries a week on television, good documentaries. All that's gone and there's very little serious documentary work done on television. I don't think people take television very seriously now, nor do they watch it for long periods; it's sort of background, or a light amusement and they maybe get their news from it, but even the news is in very quick bites. Theatre has taken over that role. I think that people rather like coming to the theatre and spending two hours really examining an issue, listening to the arguments and coming to their own conclusions. I think the same happens with film and I think we're the two media that can offer that.

That said, each of these inquiry plays – except *Guantanamo*, which wasn't strictly an inquiry play anyway – have been broadcast by the BBC, either on radio or on television. They find their way there. In fact, on the first day of the Hutton Inquiry, Geoffrey Robertson had to make the case for the inquiry being televised on behalf of ITV and Sky. Geoffrey felt it was very important and came up with nine points as to why it should be televised, and his ninth point – which he delivered with a bit of a flourish – was along the lines of: 'Your Lordship, whether you like it or not, your inquiry will be televised because it's very likely that a small theatre in North West London, who has often used actors such as Sylvia Syms who played Margaret Thatcher, and your Lordship will no doubt be played by some famous actor, will do it on the stage, and then it is likely to land up on the BBC, and I would suggest to you that it would be better if it was televised at first hand rather than at second hand.' Well, it's nice to be used as a legal argument. Lord Hutton didn't give way, but he did land up being played by an actor when the play was televised by the BBC.

HAMMOND

Does it make sense for a verbatim play to be reviewed by a theatre critic, rather than, say, a political journalist?

KENT

I think the theatre critics go into another mode. They're much more circumspect. They're a little unsure; they want to know the background to the play because they know they'll be judged by other columnists in the newspaper. The political editor might come along and say, 'Oh, this is all rubbish, this isn't true at all', or, 'This is very important, and why has no one else thought of this?' When we were doing *Called to Account*, there were a lot of questions from the critics before they went in as to the legal position; they wanted to be very sure, because they were dealing with fact. They wanted to know whether Tony Blair actually could be indicted and under what law, and how this indictment could happen.

There's an enormous amount of curiosity from the critics about this sort of work; they're very supportive of it in many ways because they see theatre engaging with the public in a wider context. I think there's a desire from the critics for theatre to be making the news, which is as it should be.

STEWARD
Does it help that the plays have been edited by someone who is a journalist, rather than a playwright? Do you think Richard Norton-Taylor is in an unusual position?

KENT
I think Richard lends a serious credibility to the plays, but I think his work shouldn't be underestimated either. His whole motivation is to try to be as objective as possible and to eschew bias – and to tell a story succinctly. He's got an incredibly clear mind. A playwright would approach things differently, that's absolutely true.

HAMMOND

Do you think a tribunal play could reach a level of such artistry that it transcends its material and attains a broader, more artistic significance?

KENT

It's an interesting question. I wouldn't ever claim to have an overarching metaphor in one of my plays, and I'm not so certain that verbatim theatre will become a classic form; I'm not expecting these plays to last. They're a response to a moment. I'm not looking at them as art, I'm looking at them as a journalistic response to what is happening.

I got into this sort of theatre when I staged transcripts of the *Romans in Britain* trial for the Oxford Playhouse Company. Each evening we performed transcripts of the trial that day, and there was a whole hearing at the Old Bailey as to whether we were in contempt of court by doing so. It seemed ludicrous that you could report court proceedings in a newspaper but you couldn't play them out on a stage, but the judge closed the court and held a hearing as to whether we were in contempt, and eventually ruled that we were not. We were the first people ever to put a trial on stage as it took place.

I would say that David Hare was an important early influence in verbatim theatre and we've sort of leapfrogged each other. He saw, and championed, Richard's *Colour of Justice*, because he felt – and he's on public record as saying – it was appalling that it was not nominated as Best Play that year at the *Evening Standard* awards. To his mind it was the most important play of that year, which was a very generous compliment from one writer to another. David said that *The Colour of Justice* stimulated his interest in verbatim again.

Then when I saw *The Permanent Way*, I had been thinking of doing *Guantanamo* for quite some time, as an opera in fact. Both ENO and the Royal Opera House wryly dismissed the project. Then I saw *The Permanent Way* and I thought, 'If David Hare can do this about the railway, surely I can put something together about Guantanamo.' That evening I phoned Gillian Slovo and asked if she'd switch from another verbatim project I'd commissioned, on immigration, to *Guantanamo*. So out of *The Permanent Way* came *Guantanamo*, so everyone is informing each other's work, and that's the excitement of good theatre.

When we did *Nuremberg* there was an extraordinary moment. Richard had carefully chosen to present the main architects of Nazism. We had Goering, the deputy; Keitel, the head of the army; Speer – the architect; Rosenberg, who'd rationalised and defended the final solution; and Hess, who had given evidence about the running of Auschwitz. It was very intense and there were one or two people there who had actually reported at Nuremberg and who said that it felt so like being in the courtroom – for instance, Ralph Koltai, the theatre designer who had been a translator at Nuremberg, and Gitta Sereny who had also been there. But there was a moment at the end, after two hours of listening to these men, when Goering was allowed to make a final statement in his own defence. And in the middle of it one night, a rather elderly woman with a German accent – obviously a refugee from the Second World War – started to shout out, 'Don't listen to him, it's all lies, lies, he's just telling lies!' She was standing up, shouting at him and persuading the audience not to listen. And then she suddenly realised she was in the theatre and she just sat down and started to cry. It was a terrifying moment because one doesn't want to reawaken that in anyone. But I think it encapsulated the power of this sort of theatre: that it is so near the truth, and actually people respond to it in a completely different way, because they feel not only moved and engaged, but they feel there's an argument that's being made, an argument they might dislike or even hate, and they feel empowered to argue back.

Audiences will hiss people, they will cheer people. I always remember people clapped Andrew MacKinlay, who was the man who came up with the quotation in *Justifying War* comparing David Kelly to chaff. When I watched him give evidence at the inquiry, he came over to begin with as a slight buffoon, and then you realised what sense he was talking – the way he analysed what had happened and what Kelly's function had been, closing down the argument about the dossier. As a Member of Parliament he felt he hadn't really been allowed to understand fully the arguments for going to war because of the way the intelligence had been handled. When the actor playing him came on stage and started talking, everyone rather laughed at him because he was sort of pompous, as he bumbled away. But gradually they were won over by his arguments, and he was the one person who almost every night the audience would applaud as he left, not because of the actor's performance but because of what he had said.

In the Lawrence play, at the end of the inquiry, when we'd listened to all the evidence, the judge said to the lawyers – not the audience; the people on stage – he said, 'In conclusion, before

I close this inquiry, I would like you to stand for a minute in memory of Stephen Lawrence and his family's fight for justice.' And the entire audience used to stand. Not because he'd actually asked them, but they felt that having listened to the evidence they were involved in what that family had gone through and the way they had been treated, and they wanted to show respect to the family, and they stood.

INDEX